June 2

To: Shirley Collier

wishing health,
happiness & prosperity
in all you do.

Proposal Writing

to **WIN**

Federal Government and National Laboratory Contracts

By Joseph R. Jablonski

Published by
Technical Management Consortium, Inc.
Albuquerque, New Mexico, USA

4

Published by:
Technical Management Consortium, Inc.
1708 White Cloud NE
Albuquerque, New Mexico 87112, USA

ISBN (13) 978-1-878821-12-6
ISBN (10) 1-878821-12-1

Five-Phase Approach™ is a registered trademark of Joseph R. Jablonski

Figures 21 - 24, Pages 209 - 213, Copyright © 24 Hour Company, Falls Church, Virginia. Reprinted with permission.

Special appreciation to
Carole Jablonski, editor & administrative assistant
Margo Bouchard, editor & desktop publisher
Laura Tuele, cover design

First Printing, April 2007
10 9 8 7 6 5 4 3 2 1
Printed in the United States of America

Dedication

To my sons Joey Jr. and Michael,

There is no greater joy for a father than to watch his son grow from student to teacher. Thank you, Joey, for all your help.

2LT Michael Jablonski, USMA Class of 2007 and Army Aviator. Congratulations on completing this major life milestone!

Love, Dad

Contents

Preface

Writing proposals can be exciting! With zero in-basket time and the pressure of creating a product on a constrained timeline, the process has an energy and focus some people thrive. For others, writing proposals can be a nightmare.

The goal of this book is to introduce you to a realistic, achievable process for writing WINning, competitive proposals to secure contracts with any agency of the federal government and national laboratories. It describes how to hone in on those organizations that use your products and services; establish a presence, tailor your solution to their specific needs, reduce frustration and overtime through focused efforts, maximize your business strengths and overcome its weaknesses. This book will teach you to write less while you WIN more contracts and sleep better at night.

The government marketplace is unique. It is also extraordinarily difficult to write a book on proposal writing due to the government's endless laws, regulations and rules. The government's subtle variability from agency to agency, and interpretation of their contracting directives, further complicates this challenge. This book focuses on the federal government and national laboratory marketplace. It is best to be trained to deal with the worst case scenario so you are in a superior position when submitting proposals at the federal, lab, or even the state, or municipal levels. All of the concepts, and much of the vocabulary, remain the same.

Proposal writing is frequently more challenging than an Olympic competition. In the Olympics you have three chances to WIN; a bronze, a silver, or the coveted gold. In proposal writing it is typically the gold or nothing. The challenge is to assimilate a tremendous amount of information in a compressed timeframe. You invest long hours while stimulating your creative juices to persuade the reader you are the one who should WIN. It's a huge undertaking in organizational, decision-making and knowledge management. An additional challenge is harnessing the specialized skills of the appropriate subject matter experts (SME) for those select contributions that only they can provide.

The good news is that these skills can be acquired and that you can actually improve and master them with practice. You only need a proven approach to help you navigate through this complex topic and make the best use of your valuable time.

Many small businesses dive into proposal writing as if driving a car with an accelerator with only an on-or-off switch. Either they're charging ahead full bore or initiating a panic break to make the next turn while second guessing their intent to bid. They use no roadmap, and as a result they tarnish their reputation in the eyes of the very organization they are trying to court, while pursuing business they have little chance of WINning. During this futile process they burn out their most valuable resource, their staff, forgetting they will soon need those very same people in an upcoming must-WIN procurement.

This book will address the important topic of whether you should bid or not bid an upcoming contract and several other topics that will surface after learning the inner workings of the proposal evaluation process.

This book offers a proven Five-Phase Approach^{TM} to help you decipher the myriad of government requirements and carve your way through to a successful proposal. This book will answer your most pressing questions with examples you can put to use today. It will introduce you to trends on new and emerging requirements. This will vastly improve your response time to some of these new, demanding challenges and help prevent those last minute surprises.

Even though proposal writing is challenging and a roller coaster of emotions, there are several good reasons for tackling it. First of all, the threat of running out of billable work can be a powerful motivator. Moreover, there is a sparkle and energy in everyone who wants to grow a business. It is a very special person who assumes the responsibility of securing meaningful work for his/her employees. This role further singles you out as a very special person who assumes the challenges others often avoid.

There is a great deal of satisfaction in doing work for the government. The prestige of competing for and WINning a government contract boosts your morale and reputation. Although the manufacturers of cutting-edge aircraft seem to capture the front page of our local newspapers, behind that major contract is an army of thousands of smaller companies. These small companies provide parts, procedure manuals, scientific studies, staffing, janitorial services, office supplies, and a host of other products and services that enable that front page project to successfully reach fruition. When your business is one of those supporting companies, the success of that new aircraft shines its spotlight on you. This carves another little notch in your company's belt and bumps up your firm to a better position in line for the next and bigger contract. The opportunities are boundless. Good luck!

Acknowledgements

I'd like to thank the following people who helped me in a myriad of ways in the development, preparation, and review of this book.

J. Howard Mock, Chairman and CEO of Jaynes Corporation, for allowing me to use their construction story on leadership, employee safety and delivering affordable solutions to the government.

Colleen Jolly, Principal in 24 Hour Company, who so generously contributed her time when this book was in its infant stages.

Lastly, I would like to thank Richard Trask; friend, colleague and mentor. Thank you for investing so much of your valuable time to help develop and review my book. The compressed timeline must have seemed like "one more proposal."

Book Reviewers

Richard Trask
Joey Jablonski, Jr.
Mary Curry
Robert Fisher

Thank you all

JOSEPH R. JABLONSKI

Joseph Jablonski has worked for such notable consulting firms as Booz, Allen, Hamilton. He formed Technical Management Consortium, Inc., in 1990 to apply quality management practices as a competitive positioning tool for government and private sector contracts. As a consultant to industry and government, he successfully led proposal teams to secure competitively bid contracts in a wide variety of disciplines, including high technology, professional services, hardware design and prototyping, test & evaluation, electrical contracting, office furniture, Just-in-Time (JIT), and staff augmentation. Also, he assisted one client to become one of 13 remaining strategic suppliers to Ford Motor Company—out of 300 initial competitors.

He has authored more that 24 technical and management reports and 5 books. One book became a best-seller and is endorsed by Stephen R. Covey, author of the immensely successful *The 7 Habits of Highly Successful People*. As a certified Master Instructor, he has developed and delivered technical and management programs to widely diverse audiences including college students, adult learners, and civilian and military leaders in government and industry throughout the U.S., Canada, and Mexico.

Joseph received his B.S. and M.S. degrees in Mechanical Engineering from the University of New Mexico, and is listed in *Who's Who in U.S. Executives* and the *International Who's Who in Quality*. He is a certified, Level III Acquisition Professional, specializing in Science & Technology and a member of the *Association of Proposal Management Professionals* (APMP).

Chapter 1.0   Introduction

1.1 Why Pursue Government Contracts?

When the famous bank robber Jesse James was finally captured, the sheriff asked him why he robbed all those banks. Jesse quickly replied, "Because that's where the money is." So, at the most elemental level, companies pursue government contracts because, in Jesse's words, "that's where the money is."

The machinery of government requires a lot of hard working, dedicated specialists to ensure that the functions of government are carried out in a timely, cost-effective manner. One way to accomplish this is by *outsourcing* business functions traditionally assigned to government officials, civil servants, or military personnel. In these times of constrained budgets and manpower, outsourcing has become a popular alternative. The United States Government procures hundreds of billions of dollars in products and services annually from leasing equipment, tradeoff studies of engineering systems, evaluating the pros and cons of placing a new weapon on the battlefield, purchasing computers and networking equipment to streamline the General Services Administration (GSA); and a host of other products and services. If you can imagine what a city, a business, a university, or a research laboratory could possibly need, chances are the government purchases it as well.

The federal government alone awards more than 11 million contracts each year with $275 billion going to small businesses in the form of direct contracts with the government or as a subcontractor to the government through a prime contractor. Ninety-nine percent of these successful companies have fewer than 500 employees. Many of them are literally mom and pop firms delivering a product or service they can uniquely provide, or in some cases, theirs was the only company willing to put forth the effort to apply! Despite the lucrative opportunities offered by government contracts, only 5 percent of American companies choose to take advantage of them, mainly because the intricacy of government rules, regulations, and public laws intimidate even the strong at heart. Yet other companies, that successful 5 percent, view the federal marketplace as a logical place to grow and diversify their business base.

One large company, Booz, Allen, Hamilton, had a thriving business in the private sector with impressive fees. But along with the high fees came very demanding assignments that ranged from days to months in duration, presenting innumerable hiring and retention challenges for management. For this firm, moving into multi-year government contracts proved to be a successful direction for growth. It ensured a more stable, long-term client and income base. One small company, a training firm in Colorado Springs, Colorado, tripled their staff overnight, from 30 to 90 employees, when they won their first training contract with Ft. Carson Army Base just south of Colorado Springs. They provided training to active-duty military and recalled reservists on basic military skills, such as driving a Humvee with night vision goggles, firing an M-4 rifle, and other life-saving skills.

In time of war, the products and services you deliver assumes an increased level of importance. Behind every man and woman we send into harm's way there is a long trail of companies, both large and small, tending to their needs. Whether it's toothpaste, software modification to a radar system, advanced avionics or perimeter security guards to supplement the military, you are providing valuable goods or services. Your company can help ensure victory in the global war on terror and ensure our young men and women return home safely. What you provide as a government contractor is important, and the government could not function without you.

The purpose of this book is to translate these volumes of complex rules and procedures into a digestible form. You can use this knowledge to your advantage in this important, competitive arena.

1.2 What is a Small Business?

There are many applications for small business in government contracting. For instance, small businesses provide the truly innovative ideas and are agile enough to respond when a course of action is not fruitful. The Small Business Administration (SBA) defines a small business as a concern that is independently owned and operated and not dominant in its field of operation. What constitutes a small business in your case varies widely from industry to industry. A brief excerpt from the SBA Size Standards is included in Table 1.

As you can see in Table 1, the standards for small business size are matched to the North American Industry Classification System (NAICS) Codes. Size standards are expressed according to annual sales receipts or number of employees. You can look up the size standard that applies to the industry your company serves by clicking on the following link.

http://www.sba.gov/size/indextableofsize.html

Having one or more NAICS Codes is an early step to becoming a government contractor. Your NAICS Codes are an important means for the government to "find you" when performing a *market analysis* for an upcoming procurement.

Table 1. SBA Table of Small Business Size Standards

NAICS Codes	NAICS U.S. Industry Title	Millions of dollars	Number of employees
541310	Architectural Services	4.5	
541710	Research & Development in Physical, Engineering and Life Sciences		500
541330	Engineering Services	4.5	
336414	Guided Missile and Space Vehicle Manufacturing		1000
322222	Coated and Laminated Paper Manufacturing		500
236118	Residential Remodelers	31.0	
221330	Steam and Air Conditioning Supply	11.5	
238160	Roofing Contractor	13.0	

As you also can see in the table, a small company is sometimes not so small. The threshold for an architectural firm is $4.5 million in fees per year. Conversely, a company manufacturing guided missiles and space vehicles can be classified as small if they have fewer than 1000 employees. If your company is about to exceed its size standard and become a large company, these standards have important implications for how you decide to develop your business. Once you exceed the small business threshold you will compete head to head with the behemoths in the government contracting marketplace—giant companies like Northrop Grumman, SAIC, and others. There is no middle ground. If you are approaching the size standard for your industry you can refine your calculation of annual sales or number of employees by referring to the following *Federal Acquisition Regulation* (FAR) Clauses: 13 CFR 121.104 and .106.

1.3 How to Use This Book

The newcomer may use this book to gain a basic understanding of the concepts and vocabulary of government contracts in order to make the best use of his and his potential clients' time as they pursue a budding relationship with a new agency. The seasoned professional may use this book to sharpen his or her skills and gain an appreciation of how others conduct business in industries both similar and different from his own.

This book may be used in two ways. You may read it from cover to cover or use it as a quick reference guide, reading the chapter or section that fills your immediate needs or interests. If you are new to government contracting, you might read this book during a coast-to-coast airline flight before getting started on your proposal. Or, if you are confronted with the clock ticking as you approach the due date for your first proposal, you might prefer to use this book as a quick reference source.

To learn how the government develops its requirements and whether or not you can influence that process, go straight to Chapter 4, Government RFP Development. If you are only interested in marketing to government and identifying the appropriate government point of contact for any upcoming professional service contract, you will find what you need in Chapters 5 and 6, Marketing to Government and Preparing to Receive the RFP. If you just received a Request for a Proposal (RFP) and are looking for pointers to help you secure SME input to get a WINning proposal completed on time, go directly to Chapters 8, 9 and 10, Proposal Development. If you just scheduled a proposal debrief with your client and would like to better prepare for this important meeting, turn to Chapter 12, Contract Negotiations and Proposal Debrief. In whatever part of the business development process you are involved, you will find helpful pointers embodied within these pages.

Chapter 2.0 Government Contracting Basics

This section is intended to introduce a working vocabulary that will be applied throughout the book. Familiarity with this vocabulary will make it easier for you to communicate with government officials, who have all received rigorous training in these terms and concepts. The same concepts will apply when working with the national laboratories, but in addition, labs have their own vocabulary. Once you decide to do business with a particular lab, you will find the specific terms they use by going to their web site or calling their Small Business Office.

2.1 What is a Contract?

A *contract* is an agreement between two parties, in this case, your firm and the government. If you happen to be a *subcontractor* to the government through a *prime contractor*, the contract with the government will be directly with the prime contractor with you in a prime-subcontractor relationship. In either case, the following terms still apply. A contract establishes a legal relationship between two parties and it defines the rights and responsibilities of each party, with provisions for making changes to the contract if needed in the future. To be binding, a contract must have five ingredients:

1. Offer

2. Acceptance

3. Consideration

4. Legal

5. Binding

An *Offer* - The offer is the proposal you prepare, sign, and submit to the government.

Acceptance - The acceptance is made by the government's representative, typically the Contracting Officer (CO) or Contract Specialist (CS), who has the authority to sign on behalf of government and, therefore, commit the government to expend federal funds.

Consideration - Consideration is typically the monies government agrees to electronically transfer into your account based upon the terms of your contract. Regardless of the type of contract you have, you will probably request monthly progress payment in your proposal to help ease your cash flow burden. In more complex contracts, part of your consideration may be your entitlement to receive a patent on work you performed for the government or the right to use proprietary results on future projects.

Legal and *Binding* - The contract becomes legal and binding when both parties have signed the contract, and thereupon it will stand up in a court of law.

2.2 Federal Acquisition Regulation (FAR)

The *Federal Acquisition Regulation*, or FAR, as it is commonly called, is a system of regulations that establishes the policies and procedures for the government's acquisition of products and services. The FAR serves as the primary source of authority to govern the procurement process and is applied across all agencies of the federal government. As mentioned above, 950 out of 1000 U.S. companies choose not to do business with the federal government. One driving reason is the FAR, which numbers 1900 pages in two volumes. Browsing this important document gives the newcomer to government contracting an appreciation for the idiosyncrasies and nuances of doing business with government. That's the bad news. The good news is that once you master the FAR in one agency of government you can directly apply this knowledge throughout all agencies of the federal government. The FAR can be reviewed at the following website:

http://www.arnet.gov/far/

As a government contractor, national laboratories are also guided by the FAR. Even if you believe yourself to be in a prime contractor role with a lab, you would be described in your contract as a subcontractor to the government through your contract with the lab. The lab may use the FAR as a guiding document, but impose commercial practices that could vary widely from what's called out in the FAR. Be advised there are two kinds of national laboratories, those that are managed by a private company and those managed by a university. For instance, Sandia National Laboratories is managed by a private company, Lockheed Martin, as a prime contractor, through a contractual relationship with the Department of Energy (DOE). Conversely, Berkeley Laboratory is managed by the University of California. This distinction has major implications for you, especially when negotiating with labs before contract award. Typically, private company-run labs are more likely to apply *Best Commercial Practices* in their procurement operations, resulting in smaller, more concise RFPs. Labs run by universities are usually, but not always, operated along the lines of how the federal government does business. Hence, universities often have voluminous RFPs that closely resemble what you encounter in government. Be advised that at this point in time all of government is making great strides to simplify the paperwork associated with their smaller procurements.

When you read an RFP for the first time, it can be intimidating reading page after page of contract clauses that are quoted from the FAR. For the small business it can be daunting trying to decipher what all these clauses mean. While you won't see my description below in any government document, it has served me well to communicate to a small company which clauses to focus on when reading an RFP. To this end, I have read three basic types of clauses:

1. Highly relevant to *YourCompany*

2. Obvious

3. The 'Red Herring'

An example of the *highly relevant* clause is FAR Subpart 15.404-4. In this type of clause the FAR provides guidance on how to calculate the profit or fee you will add onto your costs to deliver a bottom line price for your product or service. This clause is important in that, if you do go into negotiations with the government before contract award, this is a likely topic of negotiation. So much of this FAR guidance is subjective and, therefore, subject to interpretation. If you enter into discussions with a working understanding of this clause it will greatly strengthen your negotiating position.

An example of an *obvious* clause is Equal Employment Opportunity (FAR Subpart 2.2.1). In this clause, if you're awarded a government contract, you're agreeing not to discriminate because of an employee's race, color, or place of natural origin. Here government, through the FAR, is reiterating the laws of the land concerning discrimination. When you come across this type of clause, nod your head in agreement, but don't spend much time on it.

The third example, the *red herring*, can be a tremendous time-waster for anyone when they stop to ponder the meaning of this type of clause while the clock is ticking toward the proposal due date. An example of a red herring is Convict Labor (FAR Subpart 52.222-03). In this clause the government states that if you buy office furniture during the time your contract is in effect, you are encouraged to consider buying office furniture from prison labor. When you see a clause "encouraging" you to do something, you should swiftly read past it and just conclude this is something with which you may comply with.

2.2.1 Hierarchy of the FAR

When you read an RFP you may notice the agency citing lots of FAR-like guidance. This is because, while the published FAR is the starting point, the agency awarding you a contract may have its own tailored interpretation of FAR guidance. This guidance may be "reintegrated" or clarified at each level within the agency's chain of command. For instance, if you're reading an RFP to do business with the Air Force Research Laboratory, that chain will begin with the FAR itself, with additional clarifications at the Department of Defense (DOD) level, the Department of the Air Force level, the Air Force Material Command level and lastly the Air Force Research Laboratory level, the level of the organization with which you are contracting.

What is significant in these various levels of interpreting the FAR is that the FAR itself merely serves as a starting point. Somewhere in the chain of command any particular agency may have a stricter interpretation of the FARs requirements specifically tailored to its own needs. It's important that you read those interpretations of the FAR, because any one clause could be more stringent than the FAR itself and become a point of contention when you're deciding whether to bid that contract.

2.3 Government People in the Process

A question frequently asked by newcomers to government contracting is, "So whom do I speak with to discuss upcoming contract opportunities?" There are many answers to this question depending on the product or service you are delivering. To simplify, there are two basic kinds of people you may interact with. They are

1. Contracts people

2. Program people

Contracts people are the individuals in the government *Contracting Office*. They include the *Contracting Officer* (CO), *Contract Specialist* (CS), the *Buyer*, and the *Small Business Specialist* (SBS).

In the *Program Office* you may have the *Source Selection Authority* (SSA), the *Program Manager* (PM), and the *Contracting Officer Representative* (COR)—who possess the funding to initiate a contract action for products and services.

2.3.1 Contract People

In the government contracting office, the CO, CS, and Buyer all possess the authority to commit government funds, although at different levels. The Buyer may have the authority to sign off on purchases up to $25k. These are typically contracts for *commercially available off-the shelf* (COTS) items, which are frequently awarded based solely upon low price. The CO and CS have the ability to commit the government to larger procurements that may be in the millions or hundreds-of-millions-of-dollars range. On large procurements, it is typically the CS who assembles the procurement package for review before the CO signs off on the *solicitation* before release and ultimately the contract. A document called a *warrant* specifies the level of signature authority possessed by contracts personnel to commit the expenditure of federal funds.

The last person I will describe in the Contracting Office is the SBS. This individual is arguably the most important contact for the small business aspiring to do business with the federal government or national laboratory. This person works in the *Small and Disadvantaged Business Utilization Office (SADBU)*. It is the SADBUs and SBSs responsibility to ensure congressionally mandated goals for the award of government contracts to small businesses have been met. These goals include an extensive list of small business set-asides such as

- **Small Business**

- **Disadvantaged Small Business or 8(a) Contractor**

- **HUB Zone**

- **Woman-Owned Small Business**

- **Veteran-Owned Small Business**

- **Service Disabled Veteran Owned Small Business (SDVOSB)**

It should be noted that this list of set-asides is not complete. If you go to the FAR Subpart 19.5 to find out whether your company is eligible for one or more of these set-aside categories, you should know that some of these set-aside designations are self-certifying while others are not. My company is a veteran-owned small business and it is self-certifying. That means when I submit a proposal for work (an offer), I merely sign the Representations and Certifications Section of my submission, verifying my status as a veteran-owned small business. Other categories, such as

Disadvantaged Small Business or 8(a) Contractor (FAR Paragraph 252.219-7009, 8(a) Direct Awards) are not self-certifying. They undergo a rigorous certification process through the SBA. This process can result in the SBA issuing a letter to the business indicating that they are 8(a) Certified. In other cases, when the government anticipates an upcoming contract will be an 8(a) set-aside, these companies may need to submit their certifying letters in advance of RFP release.

The SADBU should be a new small business's first stop when marketing to government. They can answer the basic questions such as, "Do you buy what I sell?" "Who is the person in your organization who uses what I sell?" and, "Do I fit into any of your small business set-aside categories?" It's the SBS in the SADBU office who can best advise you on whom to contact in the Contracting Office or a particular Program Office within the organization. Depending on what you sell, you may network with people in the Contracting Office, a Program Office, or both. This topic is so important that we'll discuss it further in Section 5.3.1.

The importance of the SBS role in providing you with a first contact with any relevant agency of government cannot be overstated. One of the best descriptions of what these people do was delivered by a woman SBS from Brooks Air Force Base in San Antonio, Texas. She said, "Twenty-five percent of my job description includes working face-to-face with small businesses, and it occupies 90 percent of my time." In a typical government organization with a few thousand employees you may have one SBS, assisted only by a receptionist, so their time is very valuable. Therefore, it is best to make the best use of their valuable time by demonstrating that you have done some preliminary research on how to do business with their organization. This can be done by performing a Google search of their organization on the Internet. When you find their home page, basic questions such as what they buy, how they buy it, points of contact and the like, can easily be obtained from their website, so by the time you first meet with the SBS you should have a sense of whether they use your product or service. The SBS can then help you identify the specific points of contact within their organization to follow-up and begin making a sale.

Having said all that about the SBS in the federal government, let's look at how that differs when doing business with a national laboratory. In sharp contrast to the austere government office with one or two people, the labs typically have a much larger staff to interface with small business. Although it would certainly be wise to spend some time on their website determining the same information we discussed above, the specifics of whom to speak with, their job titles, and applicable procurement vocabulary is best learned during a face-to-face meeting with the SBS. The labs have far more people to provide this first interaction with your firm.

In your first conversation you want to determine how they're organized. Some labs have small business representatives within a centralized small business office who are assigned to particular commodities or to a specific category of product or service. In other labs, these people are in a separate, decentralized small business office, bringing you closer to the ultimate end user of what you sell. Here, the SBS may be replicated by a Division or a Business Enterprise Area specialist with a thorough knowledge of how your product or service may be used throughout their specific part of the lab's operation. The centralized contact is preferable if you are selling COTS products and services that can likely be used by all divisions such as office equipment and perimeter security.

If the lab has decentralized SBSs in each major Division, it is preferable if you deliver complex products or services, such as engineering services or software development. Clearly, under the decentralized model, you need to invest considerably more time networking to discover the precise person who buys what you sell, and learn his needs and buying patterns. The advantage of this kind or organizational structure is that each Divisional SBS has a much greater understanding of his particular division's needs and, hence, should be able to help create a better match between your company and those who will actually use your product or service. At this point the decision maker who buys what you sell is typically a Program or Project Manager and is responsive to your questions.

2.3.2 Program People

Program People are those who are responsible for buying and developing new products and services for government, and for bringing cutting edge technologies to their customers. For the Internal Revenue Service (IRS) this could be a next-generation computer system to speed up processing of your tax refund. For the National Institute of Health (NIH) it could be transitioning to electronic records management, and for the DOD, it could be delivering speedier healthcare to our troops in harm's way. There are typically three basic types of personnel in the Program Office with which you should be familiar

1. Source Selection Authority (SSA)

2. Program Manager (PM)

3. Contracting Officer Representative (COR)

If you have an existing contract with the government agency to which you anticipate delivering a proposal, the SSA is probably the person sitting in the center seat in the first row during quarterly or semi-annual program review meetings. The SSA is the major decision maker for one or more of the Program Managers within his or her sphere or responsibility. For example, if the SSA is the Director for Aircraft Renovations at Tinker Air Force Base in Oklahoma City, he or she may have individual PMs for each aircraft type they refurbish. Furthermore, they may have PMs responsible for developing new hardware and software to increase capability for modifications being installed on aircraft a year or two in the future. The point is, there are any number of PMs with whom you may network depending on whether you selling fasteners or the next-generation software for integration into new avionics boxes presently under development.

These PMs are responsible for managing requirements, budgets, and schedules for their projects, i.e., to refurbish or upgrade aircraft. In addition, there is an additional kind of PM. This PM is responsible for managing the contract action that begins with identification of a requirement that needs to be satisfied to keep a part of the facility performing its important function. This PM has the responsibility of identifying a new or recurring requirement when the existing contract is about to expire, and to work closely with Contracts to have a new RFP distributed and contract awarded in a timely manner. This PM may also be the person in charge of funding the new contract with overall management of contract execution after the award of the contract.

The Contract Officer Representative, or COR, is responsible for day-to-day interactions with the contractor and the management of the contract in close liaison with the Contracting Office. As is frequently the case, the PM responsible for managing the solicitation commonly becomes the COR after contract award. This important person is the one who receives your monthly invoices and verifies they are reasonable before sending them on to Contracts for ultimate payment by Defense Finance and Accounting System (DFAS), or whatever organization your client uses for payment. If there is a need to modify the existing contract, say for costing a change to the contract, the COR coordinates this change, or contract modification (Mod), through Contracts.

2.4 What Government Buys

Government agencies and national labs buy products and services to satisfy two basic kinds of requirements:

1. ### Products and services to run a "Small City"

2. ### Products and services to support the organization's Core Functions

Understanding whether your company supports an organization's Small City Services or Core Functions can play an important role in determining with whom you network to position yourself for an upcoming contract. This topic is important and is discussed in the following paragraph.   Figure 1 lists an example of how one national laboratory organizes its procurement actions.

Figure 1. Commodities Acquired via Sandia Laboratories Procurement Organization

Architecture/Engineering & Construction Services and Real Property Leases - All effort for mobile offices, pre-fabricated buildings, or a Real Property Lease; Architect/Engineering and construction services (subject to Davis Bacon Act), office or laboratory furniture, repair and maintenance of real property.

Research & Development Studies - All effort to support studies devoted to Research & Development, Demonstration, Feasibility, Task Performance, Design, Development, Test, Experimentation, Data Gathering, Analysis, Investigation, and Literature Search. Furnish or deliver data, first Article, Research Paper, Custom Software, Code, Experiment Results, Test Results, Information, Report, or resultant non-commercial product or prototype.

Manufacturing: Build/Fabricate to Sandia Design - All effort to fabricate, make or build to print, drawing or specification. Any reference to machining, manufacturing, plating, painting, or assembly, Circuit Boards or (Printed Wiring Boards (PWB) or Printed Circuit Boards (PCB).

Support Services & Staff Augmentation - Custom services to maintain or operate specific functions or capabilities located at Sandia Labs. These services include both contractor-directed and Sandia-directed work. In addition, the department is responsible for procurement of staff augmentation services, consultants, speakers, and miscellaneous professional services from individuals.

Just-In-Time (JIT), Accelerated Procurement System (APS), and P-Card JIT - A purchasing system or process that permits Sandia employees to electronically purchase a line of items or services directly from a designated supplier. Materials or products range from office supplies to chemicals and services include everything from water-conditioning to pager air time. All items needed on a recurring basis. Procurement awards multi-year JIT pricing agreements.

APS - A purchasing system used to obtain small value, less than $25K Commercial of the Shelf (COTS); spot buys of commercial products and one-time services.

P-Card - A purchasing system in which the actual user or requester has the authority to make small value COTS item purchases with a Visa credit card. Limits are $5K per item and $10K per transaction. Procurement manages relationship with P-Card issuing bank.

Commercial Products and Services Procurement - Commercial product and services usually greater than $25K including: Automated Data Processing Equipment (ADPE) or Telecommunications products; maintenance agreements for ADPE equipment or for commercially available computer software; capital equipment and its maintenance, optics, machine tools, instruments, etc.

Source: http://www.sandia.gov/supplier/docs/webuy.pdf

Imagine the customer as a military installation or national lab with universal needs that must be met for everyone working in its facilities. Such needs would include perimeter security, janitorial services, cafeteria, as well as engineering services to design the extension of underground utilities or install the infrastructure for a building that will be constructed the following year. These Small City contracts may include office supplies, computer purchases and Information Technology (IT) support that will benefit everyone within the "Small City." Even if you routinely sell to colleges and universities and are now positioning yourself to sell to the Navy's premier institutions, such as the United States Naval Academy in Annapolis, Maryland, or the Naval Post-Graduate School in Monterey, California, these locations still buy and maintain such universally used systems as those for heating, ventilation, and air conditioning (HVAC), road maintenance, and the like.

Government also buys products and services necessary to support an organization's Core Functions. At the Naval Academy this may include textbooks, white boards, projectors, and any other product or service required of any institution of higher learning. For the U.S. Army this may include software development to support the design of a new laser tracking system, or a Research & Development (R&D) effort for the next generation of portable food needed to feed our troops in remote locations. For the IRS, this may be custom systems engineering studies to identify and evaluate the tradeoffs associated with the next generation of computer systems that will power the IRS in the coming decades.

There are a few notable exceptions to the generalization I have given above. These are in the areas of Architectural and Engineering (A&E), Construction, and Environmental Services. In these unique cases, the services offered could benefit everyone on the installation, but because of the technical nature of the work, there needs to be someone representing the government who can more precisely communicate requirements and oversee the quality control of your work. In these instances an A&E firm would likely interact with a PM or COR in the Construction or Public Works Office. An environmental services firm would likely have a similar relationship with someone in the Environmental Office who performs similar installation-wide support. The specifics of with whom you should communicate and network for the purposes of bidding and earning work is best determined through visits to the organization's web site and conversations with the SBS. These sources will help lead you to the right person.

In summary, if you're selling a product or service that supports running a "Small City," you're probably speaking with people in the Contracting Office. If you offer a product or service that supports Core Functions, you're probably coordinating with a PM or COR in the cognizant Program Office. This person could offer valuable insights as to how you can tailor your solution to their specific needs to give you an advantage over the competition when the next solicitation is released.

Knowing with whom to speak is a good first step in your marketing effort. One important feature that distinguishes people in the Contracting Office from people in the Program Office is their motives. The objective of contracts people is to ensure the FAR is observed and any new contract does not violate any laws guiding the government's procurement policies. They are conservative people and oftentimes difficult to obtain information from other than what is disclosed in open small business forums.

Conversely, people in the Program Office will speak to anyone who might be able to deliver something that promises to increase the capability of whatever they are working on. This is the case until *Blackout*, when the RFP or Draft RFP is released. Blackout occurs when government approaches a point in the procurement process where they don't want to give one potential bidder an advantage over another. When Blackout begins all communications between government and bidders are closely controlled through the CO or CS. While contracts managed by the contracting office are frequently low-price types of contract awards, program people prefer *Best-Value* contract awards where price is but one factor in their ultimate decision as to who will be awarded the contract.

2.5 How Government Buys Products and Services

This section will help contractors better choose which kinds of contracts they may want to pursue based on their strategic planning goals. You won't see this kind of summary anywhere else. Government purchases are based on the following three basic types of needs.

1. One-time procurement

2. Developmental procurement

3. Recurring procurement

Each offers certain advantages for the ambitious company desiring to do business with government.

One-Time Procurement - Contracts that have no obvious follow-on could be classified as one-time procurements. In other cases they fall into one of the other two categories discussed below. I recently worked with a small company wanting to respond to an RFP where the U.S. Army needed to purchase 1500 sniper scopes to support operations in Afghanistan, Iraq, and training bases here in the U.S. While I could assume the Army had purchased these items in the past and will undoubtedly purchase sniper scopes in the future, I couldn't predict when that may occur, so I would classify this as a one-time purchase. Another example of a one-time procurement would be an engineering study where it is unclear whether or not there would be interest or funding for a follow-on contract. There are historically many such one-time procurements. In the 1980's there were tradeoff studies supporting Star Wars. In the 1990's

Command, Control, Communication, Computers, Intelligence, Surveillance and Reconnaissance, or C4ISR as it was frequently called, was an area of explosive growth. The 1990's greeted us with a proliferation of IT contracts to support government's priority to connect, share information, and support federal-wide initiatives to e-commerce government transactions. Of course, government's major thrust today is Homeland Defense.

Developmental Procurement – Developmental procurement, typically associated with research studies, is a long-term effort that can result in literally decades of follow-on contract actions. As shown on Figure 2, such contracts could begin, for example, as systems engineering studies resulting in the demonstration of a new capability in hardware or as a computer simulation. If the models prove themselves through rigorous testing, this work may result in a contract to build, maintain, operate, and upgrade the product to increase capability as new technologies arise. While these contracts are traditionally reserved for large companies, it must be noted that for every large contract awarded to a Boeing or Northrup Grumman, there are many small company subcontractors delivering important services and subassemblies to make the overall system work. So as a subcontractor on these efforts you could benefit from the decades-long new contracts that emerge as the project transitions from a paper study to a working system in the field.

Figure 2. Overview of Developmental Procurement

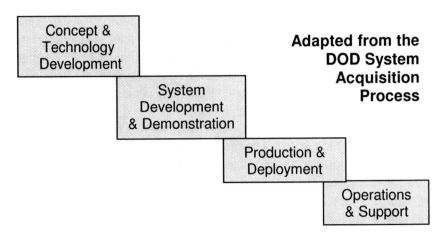

An example of a small company involved in a developmental procurement project is Honeymoon Paper, a packaging company in West Chester, OH. They received smaller contracts with the U.S. Army to develop the next generation of Made Ready to Eat (MRE) meals. MREs are single-serving meals that may be eaten hot or cold by our soldiers in the field. In this example, Honeymoon Paper conducted paper studies that resulted in a short production run of the new MREs for field testing. The resulting lessons learned helped finalize the packaging specifications allowing government to proceed onto a mass-production contract. One would expect that the company that successfully developed a new product would be uniquely positioned to WIN the follow-on production contract. So there are small company examples of developmental procurement projects—small contracts that can lead to much larger contracts later.

Recurring Contract - The third type of procurement action is the Recurring Contract. As government seeks to reduce its costs and improve delivery of services, agencies are frequently turning to contractors to outsource business functions that were traditionally classified as "inherently governmental." This opportunity has come about as the number of civilians and military in government have been reduced. Also, government's A-76 initiative to consider the cost-benefit of outsourcing work has contributed to the growth of government outsourcing. In fact, one study quoted in Defense News states that while the federal government's budget has grown modestly these past 5 years, their thrust into e-commerce has greatly contributed to the 13 percent increase in the use of professional services contracts, specifically in the area of information technology. A close second, at an astounding 11 percent per year increase, is government's use of other professional services contracts in all areas, primarily to replace government personnel.

Outsourcing has proven to be a growth opportunity for companies willing to take the plunge and work side by side with government civilians and military personnel to provide direct support of government's core functions. One such contract is the Air Force Business Resource and Support Services (BRASS) contract, which I will use throughout the book as an example of one solicitation that's indicative of today's RFPs. This 5-year, Small Business Set-Aside contract delivers support to core functions within the Space Vehicles and Directed Energy Directorates of the Air Force Research Laboratory. While government personnel manage customer funds from various federal agencies to develop new technologies, the contractor support for this core is delivered by a responsive workforce of 33 persons each year – persons employed by a small business working on this contract.

What makes this contract an especially choice opportunity for small business is that it's a recurring contract. That means you can plan when the existing contract will expire and pre-position your company to bid on the follow-on contract. It's not uncommon for an excellent, high-performing company to hold onto such contracts for decades, re-bid after re-bid. It is specifically these kinds of professional service, recurring contracts that are growth markets.

Another example is the Department of State (DOS). During a recent workshop one student was recently retired from a Regional Office of the DOS. He was hired by a small company to help oust the incumbent during an upcoming re-bid for the follow-on contract. I didn't know it at the time, but it seems the DOS has several Regional Offices, each with approximately 100 people. Twenty-five are government personnel at the core who are supported by 75 percent contract personnel to ensure smooth operation of all business functions. The market for professional support services promises to continue to grow into the foreseeable future as government continues to deliver increased value to the taxpayer via outsourcing.

2.5.1 Contracts Used to Buy Products and Services

There are many ways government purchases products and services. They range from simple on-the-spot credit card transactions for purchases of less than a few thousand dollars, to full and open competition where contract awards can range from hundreds of thousands of dollars to billions. Within these two extremes lies a host of contract vehicles used by government based upon their goals, availability of small business to perform the work, and most importantly, government's ability to find your company. One method of purchasing that can represent a competitive contract is the *Purchase Requisition*. These purchases, for routinely used products and services, are typically competitively bid by several companies with the evaluation and subsequent award being a straightforward, speedy process, most –often based upon low bid.

Within this wide range of contract vehicles there is a long list of special contracts where small businesses typically compete. Some of these special contracts are listed below:

- General Service Agency (GSA) Contracts

- Sole-Source Contracts

- Simplified Acquisitions

- Broad Agency Announcements (BAAs)

- Small Business Innovative Research (SBIRs) Contracts

- Unsolicited Proposals

- Set-Aside Contracts

GSA contracts, or Schedule Contracts as they are typically called, are a common way for companies to begin doing business with government, probably because of their ease of application, because it's a place where a company can complete, submit, and WIN a contract on their own without a lot of outside help.

A *Sole-Source Contract* is fairly unusual. Sole source means your company and your company alone can perform the work, and for that reason government should award the contract to you without competition. Every agency of government has criteria whereby they may consider a sole-source award. The list of criteria is usually lengthy, including perhaps a dozen factors that may be considered to award sole source. Probably the most frequently requested justification a PM might use to award sole source is timeliness. This generally occurs when the PM wasn't familiar with the timeline to process a solicitation through contract award. This justification is not on any list I have ever seen. Another common reason given to award sole source is compatibility when your hardware or software easily interfaces with the government's existing solution, whereby your solution can be demonstrated to be the most cost-effective choice. In today's environment, wartime urgency is a plausible justification for sole-source contract awards. In this unique case, it must be demonstrated this new contract will satisfy a direct and immediate need on the battlefield. In summary, Sole-Source Contracts represent the exception to government's routine manner of procuring goods and services and are infrequently used.

Simplified Acquisitions are for contracts of less than $1 million in value. The big advantage of receiving a contract that was processed as a simplified acquisition is timeliness. It's much faster for government to get these procurements awarded than for larger contracts. Faster means months rather than a year or more from the time the requirement for a contract was first identified through contract award.

Broad Agency Announcements (BAAs) are general announcements, typically for research work that is aligned with an agency's R&D thrusts. As the name implies, government doesn't have well-defined requirements for these new developments, but is relying on the innovation of companies and research universities to develop the next generation of an existing or new technical capability.

Small Business Innovative Research Contracts or Grants (SBIRs) are similar to BAAs in that they rely on small business ingenuity to develop technologies to known, ill-defined problems. The unique advantage of the SBIR is that it is designed to provide seed money for small business to help bring an idea to commercial fruition. These contracts are awarded in a Phase I increment up to $100k to demonstrate Project Feasibility. A Phase II follow-on of up to $750k is intended for Project or Prototype Development. Thereafter, the company is expected to rely on private investment to bring the hardware, software, or process into the commercial marketplace or through a contract directly with the government agency interested in the application of the technology.

Unsolicited Proposals are included in FAR Subpart 15.6 and describes the preparation and submission of unsolicited proposals.

Unsolicited Proposal Awards are more commonplace in the labs. Most often, if your proposal to government is unsolicited, it is unlikely money has been set aside for such an eventuality. In rare instances, where the agency has substantial end-of-fiscal-year monies to invest in promising new ideas, it may be able to fund you on short notice if your project is in line with the agency's funding priorities.

I've seen unsolicited proposals used very effectively with labs that seem to have the contractual mechanism to support new ideas. A version of unsolicited proposal also works in government when you already have an existing contract with an agency. In this case, during routine quarterly or semi-annual project review meetings, after you've already conveyed to your customer the superb job you're doing for them, you can then recommend logical add-on or follow-on work. In this instance, you possess a unique understanding of the organization's operations, needs, and priorities. You're merely recommending more work based on your ongoing efforts. This manner is prudent marketing for any company presently doing business with government where you can offer a unique solution to a known problem.

Set-aside Contracts are contract dollars that are directed toward a particular classification of small business as described in Section 2.3.1. Government earns credit toward their small business set-asides goals in two ways: with direct contracts between you and the government or, when you help a prime contractor attain their small business goals as called out in the subcontracting plan they attached to their proposal. So, regardless of how you are involved in a contract, as a prime or subcontractor, the SADBU claims credit for small business contract involvement.

2.6 Methods of Contracting

There are two basic methods of contracting: the Fixed-Price Contract and the Cost-Reimbursement or Negotiated Contract. The Fixed-Price Contract establishes a firm price for the product or service being procured by government. The Cost Reimbursement Contract reimburses the contractor for allowable, reasonable costs incurred in executing the contract up to the contract ceiling value. Cost-Reimbursement Contracts may include cost sharing or an incentive fee for higher risk efforts or cases in which the contractor stands to gain some proprietary information from the work.

2.6.1 Indefinite Delivery/Indefinite Quantity (ID/IQ)

This contract type is growing in popularity for a wide array of products and services. It allows the government to have a contract in place even though the exact delivery date and ordering quantity are not known. Typically in new contract awards the government must know that funds are readily available in their budget to proceed to contract award. However, under an ID/IQ contract, the government only needs to have sufficient funds to pay for a baseline minimum of work. The balance of the funds, and hence the work being performed, are frequently paid for by other customers (or agencies) within government.

A colleague in Las Cruces, New Mexico, works for a company that manufactures enclosures that are mounted on movable platforms such as truck beds, trailers or ships to provide a workspace where people in the field can gather data, observe test events, hold meetings, and process data in a secure environment. When government customers worldwide need such an enclosure the government creates a Delivery Order (DO) describing their needs and "put money on the contract." This contract was awarded through a competition by White Sands Missile Range.

In the professional services arena, a company called Applied Research Associates (ARA) holds an ID/IQ contract with the Defense Threat Reduction Agency (DTRA) at Ft. Belvoir, Virginia. Any government customer can put money on DTRA's contract when they desire to have test planning, analysis, and reports written for work related to anti-terrorism and Weapons of Mass Destruction (WMD) test and evaluation. The benefit to government customers outside of DTRA is that the contract vehicle is already in place to quickly start work in weeks, rather than months or a year, and a new Task Order can to be processed immediately. The advantage to the contractor is he can maintain a high caliber of technical staff under the assumption that there will be an ongoing stream of funded work. Because of its popularity, I will use an ID/IQ contract later as my example RFP.

Table 2 summarizes the merits of both Fixed-Price and Cost - Reimbursement Contracts from both the government and contractor perspective. When reviewing this comparison we see that the risk lies with the contractor on Fixed-Priced Contracts where they must manage the work well enough to have sufficient monies remaining when the work is completed to yield a profit. In contrast, on cost reimbursement contracts, the risk lies with government where only "best efforts" are expected of the contractor. In fixed price contracts, the solicitation may come to the contractor through an Invitation for Bid (IFB) that is commonly used for work that lends itself to a fixed price because costs are predictable and well known.

The Request for Quote (RFQ) is also used on simpler acquisitions. The ever popular RFP, is used by government on more complex projects where the contractor will have to respond with more information in their proposal, such as technical and management descriptions of how they conduct business, a Price/Cost submission and perhaps an entire volume describing their Past Performance and how their proposal offers the government a low risk solution for getting the work done. An ID/IQ contract may be a Fixed-Price, Cost-Reimbursement-type Contract or both, depending on the specific delivery order being processed.

Table 2. Summary of Methods of Contracting Used by Government

	Fixed Price Type Contracts	Cost Reimbursement Type Contracts
What is promised?	Delivery of acceptable goods and services	Best efforts
When is payment?	After delivery (progress payments possible)	As costs are incurred
Cost risk to: Contractor Government	High Low	Low High
Requirements	Well-defined	Less well-defined
Contractor Fee	Fee based on efficient contract performance and cost control	Fee or formula to compensate the contractor beyond costs
Type of Solicitation	Use IFB, RFQ or RFP	RFP

IFB: Invitation for Bid, RFQ: Request for Quote, RFP: Request for Proposal

2.7 Types of Contract Awards

Government may have a Fixed-Price or Cost-Reimbursement Contract and then choose to make the contract award based on low cost or *Best Value*. Low cost contract awards typically result from IFB or RFQ solicitations, whereas best value awards are typically made where the more complicated RFP solicitation is used to gather more information on how the contractor will actually perform the work. Best value awards are commonplace on RFPs and RFQs. Sandia National Laboratories, although frequently buying COTS items, still awards best value because there is often a service component to the purchase. For instance, they may buy desktop computers, which easily lend themselves to low cost bids, but then they bundle the timeliness of service delivery and the cost of on-site maintenance to the hardware purchase. The best value award allows the lab to consider factors other than just cost when awarding these contracts. In this circumstance, it is in the lab's best judgment that an aggregate of factors, such as the contractor's past performance on similar contracts, the risk their proposal approach imparts to the lab, and, of course, bottom-line price, are all considered in Sandia's decision to award. Best value awards are also a popular method of awarding contracts throughout federal government agencies.

2.8 Trends in Government Contracting

Government buys products and services in a very dynamic environment fraught with constant change. Some of these changes are so small that if you were to read about them in an RFP this morning you could easily conclude, "I could write a paragraph or two on this quite easily." In other cases, the requirements could cause you to invest a considerable amount of time teaming with other companies, demonstrating new capability to perform work called out in the RFP or RFQ or a host of other requirements that simply cannot be dealt with during those precious few weeks you have to write a proposal. It is for that reason I chose to include this section on trends in government contracting, to give you some insights into what you may see in your next RFP before you enter that critical timeframe of writing your next proposal.

Some trends I see in today's government marketplace include

- Performance-based service contracts

- Ten-year contract awards

- Oral proposals becoming more commonplace

- Inventory management

- Leasing in lieu of purchase

- Contract bundling

- E-Commerce

- The dreaded 2-week proposal

- Past Performance as a selection factor

Performance-Based Service Contracts - We've witnessed quality and performance measurement as routine topics of conversation for decades. In America's quality movement during the 1980's, we saw the concept of measurement applied to services. As of just a few years ago, government started applying performance measurements to service contracts of all kinds from Just-in-Time (JIT) delivery of on-site computer repair and support to janitorial services, engineering services, and others. One example of professional services performance requirements is included in Table 3.

Table 3. Example of Performance-Based Requirements in a Professional Service Contract

Performance Metric	Goal or Requirement	Lowest Acceptable Threshold
Technical Results		
Data Quality	100%	95%
Risk Mitigation	Apply 100% Lessons Learned within Last 5 Years	100% on Routine Tests
Innovative Solutions	100% Solutions within Contractor Team	20% Solutions Require Support Outside Team
Management Responsiveness		
Safety	No Violations	2 Non-Reportable Incidents per year resulting in no Work Stoppage
Security	No Violations	2 Non-Reportable Incidents per year resulting in no Work Stoppage
Schedule	100% Delivery Performance	99% Delivery Performance
Resource Allocation	Appropriate personnel assigned for support	Appropriate personnel assigned for support
Cost Results		
Baseline – Award Fee	1% Variation in Budget versus Actuals	1% Variation in Budget versus Actuals
TO – Cost Plus	1% Variation in Budget versus Actuals	10% Variation in Budget versus Actuals
TO – Fixed Fee	No Cost Overruns	Cost Overrun does not result in Test Schedule Slip

What is important to note is how government divides their key parameters for measurement into three familiar categories of Technical Results, Management Responsiveness, and Cost Control. Note the second and third columns to the right on this table. Column Two represents the government's ideal goal for contractor performance. Column Three is the lowest acceptable *threshold* of performance. In theory, government could cancel the contract if your technical, management or cost performance dips below this threshold. Anyone experienced in government contracting knows how unusual it is for government to cancel a contract. But in today's environment they don't need to. If you hold a 3-year base contract with an option for an additional 2 years, government can use your lack of performance as justification to not award the option years. Moreover, derogatory performance may be recorded by your CO, CS, or COR, which can greatly affect your ability to secure future contracts, as explained in the next paragraph.

Past Performance as a selection factor - There was a time when a contractor could promise almost anything in their proposal. If there was a disagreement between your company's PM and the COR, it was often simply chalked up to a "personality conflict." Today, however, the performance measurements described above quantify your performance and it is recorded for later lookup in government and laboratory databases to review how you've performed on past and ongoing contracts. Past performance can amount to as much as 25 percent of the decision to choose the contractor for award and I've seen it weighed as heavily as equal to both the technical and management volumes of your proposal. This is serious business! At the conclusion of my live workshops I ask students to complete a critique and one of the first questions I ask is, "What will you do first upon returning to the office after completing this training?" Frequently the answer is, "Now that I understand the importance of past performance, I'm going to try to clean up my report card." To summarize, you need to remember that today's contract is tomorrow's past performance.

Ten Year Contracts – With government procurement offices downsizing, they've chosen to pursue longer term contracts, as seen in the private sector. So if you're used to selling through individual purchase requisitions, you may now see your agency moving toward blanket purchase requisitions. If you're used to seeing 2-year contracts on solicitations for your products or service, you may soon see the next generation of that procurement take the form of a 3-year base contract with two or more option years. This can represent a windfall for the company prepared to bid these larger procurements where the stakes are much higher.

Oral Proposals – These are becoming quite popular in many agencies of government. National laboratories have embraced this idea as a tremendous time saver for both contractors and themselves. Price/Cost and Past Performance volumes of your proposal are still submitted as written sections or volumes. The other volumes or sections—technical, management and proposal risk—lend themselves to oral presentations, giving proposal evaluators the privilege of asking questions as they arise or in a questions and answers (Q&A) at the end. In general, they expect your presentation to be well-rehearsed and polished. Where they expect you to stumble is during the Q&A where you may not have anticipated their questions. When I've seen oral proposals delivered to agencies of the DOD, most often they are a supplement to the written volumes. This of course increases the workload for the proposal team, who are already working long days to deliver their proposals.

Inventory Management – The private sector has long relied on Just-in-Time (JIT) contracts for the delivery of products, parts, subassemblies, and services in an effort to reduce inventory management, floor space, in-house personnel for tracking and accountability, and provide a host of other benefits. Government, to some degree and the labs to a great extent, now rely on multi-year JIT contracts to shift the responsibilities for day-to-day management of these assets to the contractor yielding a substantial savings. Los Alamos National Laboratories has about 50 JIT contracts. The advantage for you as a small business wanting to compete for government and lab work is that JIT contracts are recurring. That means that if the client has routinely bought rebar and office supplies and technical support on JIT contracts in the past, chances are he will continue to do so. Therefore, the end date on existing contracts, with the incumbent contractor, contract value and customer point of contact are well known so you can plan ahead to bid the follow-on contract.

Leasing in lieu of purchase – I recently saw this for the first time from a national lab. In the past, when the lab purchased a super computer, the installation and initial operation of the system were typically awarded to a small business, with the computer itself being provided by a large manufacturer. The small company invoiced monthly as they installed the infrastructure to support the new computer—air conditioning, power, etc. After checkout and turnover of the fully functioning system and lab acceptance, the small company then received the balance of payment. Today, with constrained funding, the lab leases the system from the small company so there are no progress payments and no balance of payment upon lab acceptance. In this new environment the small company needs substantial financing to manage the deferred cash flow, which can go on for years while the lab pays for monthly use.

Contract Bundling – The Small Business Reauthorization Act of 1997 undertook a strategy to bundle contracts. Bundling was defined as consolidating one or more procurements that previously were delivered through separate, smaller contracts. Later it was discovered that bundling actually hurt small business and in October 2002 the Office of Management and Budget (OMB) submitted a report to the President with nine specific actions the administration could take to eliminate *unnecessary* bundling. Unfortunately, government had already begun realizing the savings to them with fewer solicitations to process and fewer contract awards to administer, so bundling was here to stay. Today small companies turn to teaming to provide the robust capability to address all of the requirements that may be present in a larger, bundled contract. While some small companies are positioned to thrive in this unforgiving market, others are not and are simply overtaken by ambitious peer companies.

E-Commerce – Anyone doing business with government must register with the Central Contractor Registry (CCR) (FAR Subpart 4.11). It is through this system that government and labs can perform searches to gain insights on how many companies might possibly compete for new contract work. It's also how you are paid, via electronic funds transferred into your business account. Further, e-commerce speeds up the exchange of information through email and file downloads from Contracting Offices through Federal Business Opportunities (FedBizOpps or FBO), or other servers, to rapidly distribute RFP's, solicitations amendments, and contract award announcements. E-commerce is also one reason why the government can support the dreaded 2-week proposal.

The Dreaded 2-Week Proposal – This is becoming more popular. Many companies complain about the unreasonableness of such a short turnaround time from receipt of an RFQ/RFP to submission of their proposal. But companies that practice superb filing and organizational skills know how to extract information that will help them anticipate what might be embodied in the next solicitation, and they are at a decided advantage. This trend is becoming so pervasive that I cannot overstate the need for you to anticipate a 2-week proposal in your future. These short-turn-around proposals used to be reserved for buying COTS products and services where the details of your new proposal are merely a cut-and-splice of past submissions. Not so today. I now see the 2-week proposal timeline for professional service contracts where there is a creative dimension to developing your solution. Some examples that come to mind include a 300-day project to develop training materials for the United States Election Assistance Commission (USEAC) and developing an Artificial Intelligence (AI) algorithm so the IRS can better sort which taxpayers should be audited. More recently I saw an Air Force laboratory give 2 weeks to bid a multi-year, $10 million R&D effort. I believe this trend will continue.

Chapter 3.0 Getting Started in Business Development

There is no greater reward than knowing you are personally responsible for bringing meaningful work into your company. Your success in business development through government contracts provides an ongoing stream of billable work, job security for you and your company, and the pride of delivering a valuable product or service to the American taxpayer.

To help you achieve that goal, I've chosen to begin this chapter with a review of lessons learned—feedback from proposal evaluators who read small business proposals on a regular basis, an overview of what differentiates a company's WINning business development efforts from one that is unsuccessful, and a self-assessment tool for evaluating your company's proposal development process. We'll conclude with an overview of the Five-Phase Approach^{TM} to business development followed by a summary of the important differences between doing business with the federal government and with national laboratories. The remainder of the book will discuss details of the Five-Phase Approach^{TM}.

3.1 Lessons Learned

Any company with a meaningful process for conducting business learns from its mistakes so that it is able to deliver a superior product or service next time. This smart habit of self-improvement applies to any business process, but nowhere is it as important as in the proposal development process. That's because this one process is resource constrained. There are limited Bid & Proposal (B&P) monies to compensate people who work long hours getting a WINning proposal out on schedule. So this section focuses on creating the proposal itself, based on what I have learned from my personal experiences and discussions with both contracting and program managers in government and national laboratories. The following list represents an amalgamation of these inputs, in the hope that everyone who reads this will learn from the past mistakes of others.

- Read the solicitation from cover to cover

- Contractors don't read or understand the Evaluation Criteria

- The client knows us so we don't need to respond to all of the sections of the RFP

- A few mistakes won't matter

- The need for an internal process

Read the solicitation from cover to cover – This feedback came to me across all fronts from both government and the labs very early in my research for this book. It makes proposal evaluators angry when they must read three-fourths of your proposal only to learn that you can't perform one of the many requirements called for in the solicitation and that, in short, your company is not qualified to bid. It's essential that you read and understand all solicitation requirements so you can take necessary steps to fill in any voids in your capabilities. With teaming being such a popular subject throughout government and the labs, it's prudent to begin networking with other companies to help satisfy all requirements in your proposal; or, you might decide to hire or staff up to support this new requirement. Either way, you first have to know exactly what the government wants. Read the entire solicitation!

Contractors don't read or understand the Evaluation Criteria – The evaluation criteria are described in the last section, Section M, of the RFP. Perhaps, because this information is at the end of the RFP, companies don't realize just how important it is. The evaluation criteria are the "scorecard" by which your proposal will be evaluated. Imagine your proposal opened on the evaluator's desk with the evaluation criteria immediately to his right for easy reference. That is how it is used. The evaluation criteria should play a key role in the organization of your proposal. The easier it is for proposal evaluators to locate required information, the greater the chances they'll assign you the maximum points. Conversely, the more difficult it is to find information, the more likely you will receive fewer points.

The client knows us so we don't need to respond to all of the sections of the RFP – It's commonplace for companies who presently hold a contract with the organization they are currently bidding to conclude that previous experience with the client absolves them from explaining everything in full detail. That's dangerously wrong. The evaluators are only supposed to evaluate you on your submission, not their personal knowledge. If important material is left out of what you have written, they can deem you non-responsive and move onto the next proposal. Also, it's commonplace for the proposal evaluation team to consist of three types of people: those who are very much aware of your capabilities and standing within your industry, those who may have some experience with your industry, and those who have no experience with either your company or industry. The moral of the story is to thoroughly read the RFP from cover to cover, respond to every requirement called out in the RFP and organize your proposal submission to make it easy for the evaluators to grant you maximum points.

A few mistakes won't matter – As a small company you inevitably send out proposals with a typo or two. This is OK, your evaluators recognize you are a small company and are creating a proposal on a constrained timeline with limited resources. But if the errors exceed a certain threshold, it's easy for the client to conclude this proposal is an example of the quality you will deliver while executing the contract. So in my 17-Step Proposal Development Process in Chapter 8, I specifically include an end-to-end review of the final proposal before it goes into production and shipment to the client.

Lastly, *the need for an internal process* – Government clients often comment that on one occasion a company submits a great proposal and on another they turn in something that is obviously inferior. This compels the need for an internal set of checks and balances to ensure a certain level of quality in each and every proposal you submit. We'll review the business development process in Section 3.4. The proposal development process will be covered in detail in Chapters 8 through 10.

3.2 WINning versus Losing Business Development Efforts

In Section 3.1 we focused on what proposal evaluators see when reading your proposal. Let's step back for a moment and consider the myriad of communications and interactions between you and your perspective client. This will serve to better understand what occurs outside that brief period of time when you're writing your proposal. As we can see from Table 4, the difference between WINning and losing teams from your ability to focus on what's truly important, effective communication and how you develop and maintain relationships with potential client. We'll see how these important topics fit into the Five-Phase Approach™ in Section 3.4.

Table 4. Overview of WINning versus Losing Business Development Efforts

WINning	Losing
Ability to focus on what's truly important	No process
Interactive dialogue with clients	No dialogue
Single point of contact (POC) with client	Unfocused, not coordinated
Understanding the background and assets of key decision makers	No ongoing dialogue
Building a business relationship on trust and fulfilled promises	Inconsistent and unreliable attempts to relate

Source: Adapted from *The Difference Between Winning and Losing Capture Efforts* by Jay Herther, APMP Journal, Spring/Summer 2005.

3.3 Proposal Readiness Assessment

Before delving into the Five-Phase Approach™, it's important to understand where your company is positioned in its readiness to compete for work. Figure 3 describes a five-level stair step to follow in assessing your readiness to secure contracts. This approach is adapted from the Capability Maturity Model developed by Carnegie Mellon. Many factors distinguish a Level 5 company from a Level 1 company. Some of the key factors include employee training, a solid process for business and proposal development, and employee willingness to participate in proposal development. Understanding what level your company is at will help you assess what must be done to attain the next level.

Figure 3. Proposal Readiness Assessment

Level 5. Continuously Improving
Level 4. Predictable Results
Level 3. Established Process
Level 2. Beginning to use a Process
Level 1. Ad Hoc

The Level 5 company has an established process for getting successful proposals out the door and can generally predict whether they will win this next bid or if it's a high-risk venture due to existing company shortfalls or the level of competition. Moreover, company managers integrate lessons learned from past proposal efforts into their resource library so they are better prepared for the inevitable next proposal.   When a Level 5 company has newcomers involved in writing a proposal they sit down with these people, introduce them to the company's process for doing business, describe how all participants in the process are involved, and most importantly, inform them when they will be done with their contribution.   Also, if there are program people involved in the procurement, they understand the importance of these relationships to help you interpret what is truly important to them. The result of this refined process is that every time a Level 5 company prepares a proposal, staff becomes more proficient.

The Level 3 company has a process for proposal writing but generally doesn't understand the broader picture of how actions taken before receiving the RFP, and after proposal submission, can influence their ability to WIN. Also, if there is someone working on a proposal for the first time, the Level 3 company has this person figure out on his own the details of the process and how he will fit in as time goes by.

At the lowest level, the Level 1 company is easy to recognize. If there's even a hint of an RFP coming in, staff scatters. Long-time employees who have worked many proposal efforts before ask, "Gee, have we done this before?" So, some of the key ingredients that distinguish what level a company is at is having an established process, employee training, integration of 'Lessons Learned' into the next proposal effort, open communications and working relationships with program people, and probably most importantly, a solid Bid/No-Bid decision process. The Bid/No-Bid decision communicates to every employee that their time is valuable and management has given a great deal of thought to the decision to involve others in this time-consuming process to create a WINning proposal which everyone will be proud of. The approach to becoming a Level 5 company will be introduced in Section 3.4 and described in greater detail throughout the rest of this book.

3.4 The Five-Phase Approach^{TM} to Business Development

WINning proposals are not merely written, but are developed as an integral part of a larger business development process. Figure 4 provides an overview of the Five-Phase Approach^{TM} to a successful business development methodology. Subsequent chapters describe each phase in greater detail. The five-phases are divided into two basic categories: (1) what occurs in government and (2) what occurs in your company. What occurs in government is a mystery at best. This simple insight can help you tremendously when you are preparing to receive an RFP by making you knowledgeable about what takes place in shaping the solicitation and what transpires after your proposal is submitted. Knowing how the wheels of government turn is invaluable as you will be able to anticipate what government actions will occur and at what points you may influence the process. I frequently hear students in my workshops comment, "Gee, I wish I had known that before turning in my last proposal," or "Now I understand the significance and intent of the Pre-Award Debrief."

Figure 4. The Five-Phase Approach™ to Business Development

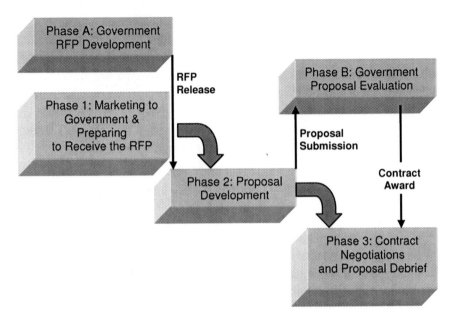

There are two phases in government: RFP Development and Proposal Evaluation as shown in Figure 4. Their titles are self-explanatory. Phases 1, 2 and 3 occur in your company.

- ## Phase 1: Marketing to government and preparing to receive the RFP

- ## Phase 2: Proposal development

- ## Phase 3: Negotiating with government and your Proposal Debrief

In Phase 1 you network with potential clients, uncover opportunities to bid and make the all-important decision to

Bid/No-Bid a particular contract. In Phase 1 you may also uncover requirements in an upcoming RFP that you simply cannot respond to in the brief few weeks you have to write a proposal. These long-lead items become tasks to be addressed in advance of receiving the RFP and will be described in detail in Chapters 5 and 6.

Phase 2 begins when you receive the RFP. Read the solicitation carefully to determine if you can reply to all of its requirements, create a detailed outline, make writing assignments, integrate all of the inputs into a concise, WINning document that clearly states, "We're the company who should receive this contract award." Phase 2 concludes when your proposal is delivered to the client. The details of the 17-Step approach to accomplish Phase 2 will be described in Chapters 8, 9, and 10.

Phase 3 begins when your proposal is evaluated and concludes when you are notified of contract award and start work. Interactions between you and government during this time may include answering questions posed by proposal evaluators, negotiating specific points in your proposal, and receiving a proposal debrief for valuable information that will help you on future proposal.

3.5 A Comparison of Doing Business with Government and National Laboratories

To this point I've used the terms federal government and national laboratories almost interchangeably. Now it's time to look at the differences that may influence your decision to pursue business with one over the other. Table 5 offers a brief comparison of conducting business with the federal government versus the national labs. In Chapter 2 I mentioned there are two basic types of national labs: those managed by a private company and those managed by a university. These two kinds of labs conduct business quite differently. The company-run lab frequently applies Best Commercial Practices to their procurement processes, whereas the university-run lab usually follows government guidelines. You first see this when thumbing through an RFP from a university-run lab and find, for example, the section headings are similar in title and number of pages to federal government RFPs. So, the two columns in Table 5 may be viewed as government and university-run labs in the left column with private-company run labs on the right.

I like working with private company-run labs because they are trend-setters in procurement. For instance, I bid my first performance-based service contract with a private company-run lab in the late 1980's. Today, in the federal government, we call them performance-based service contracts. So, performance-based service contracts have been used in some labs for almost two decades. In contract, it has only been a requirement in government for the past several years, with some government organizations implementing performance-based service contracting in the last year or two. Not only are the private-run labs the first to implement cutting-edge requirements you may see later in government, but also, labs are particularly good at providing training on new requirements.

Table 5. Comparison of doing business with the Federal Government versus National Laboratories

Government	National Laboratories
All procurement actions over $25k advertised in FedBizOpps (FBO)	Rely on in-house resources and PM knowledge, FBO a last resort
FAR and Solicitation Sections A thru M	Trend toward commercial practices with shorter, more concise solicitations
Easy for large companies to make small business goals for government through their small business plan	Small Business Office and Contracts Office work hard to make ambitious small business goals by contracting directly with small companies
Government too conservative to suggest partnering	May suggest two synergistic companies team to bid complete requirement
Some contract forecasting enabling potential bidders to plan ahead	Well defined JIT contract schedule to benefit future bidders
PM, COR well-defined roles and authority	Terminology unique to each laboratory
Oral proposals becoming more commonplace with controlled Q&A	Oral proposals very common with free-flow of information in Q&A
Your No-Bid decision may result in a letter notifying Contracts	May require you to send your intent to No-Bid in a letter to the lab to remain on in-house Bidder's List
May choose to go directly to Contract Award without Negotiations	Frequently negotiates even on allowable expenses called out in the FAR

Some noteworthy differences in Table 5 are the following:

Where procurements are advertised - According to the FAR, the federal government must advertise all procurement actions over $25k in FedBizOpps (FBO). Labs advertise through their own means. In fact, if you see a national lab advertising in FBO it's an indication they are having trouble fostering competition through their own sources and are turning to FBO as a means of increasing their pool of potential bidders.

Coaching two synergistic companies to team on an upcoming procurement - The labs are quite good at coaching small companies to team up to offer the lab a complete solution, whereas the federal government would never make such suggestions to private companies.

The no-bid decision - If you choose not to bid a solicitation you receive from the federal government, it is considered a courtesy to advise them of this. If many companies choose to notify the government they don't intend to bid, it could cause the government to re-release their RFP after gathering comments from these potential bidders. Conversely, it's a requirement that you let the labs know if you do not intend to bid a contract after they have sent you the solicitation. Since they most often rely on an in-house list of potential bidders, not letting them know your intentions not to bid can result in your being removed from their bidder's list for future opportunities.

Negotiations leading up to contract award – Negotiations are conducted quite differently by these two clients. Government is selective; for example, they most likely will negotiate on fixed price, City Products and Services contracts, but probably not on Best Value, negotiated awards. In sharp contrast, the labs will often choose to negotiate any type of contract in an effort to bring down costs. Their objective is to reduce small business contract charges by reinterpreting contract risk to reduce their fee and lining out costs you may deem to be allowable under the FAR.

Chapter 4.0 Government RFP Development (Phase A)

Chapter 4 will detail Phase A of the Five-Phase Approach™ to Business Development illustrated by Figure 4 in Chapter 3.

Phase A, Government RFP Development, begins when the need for a contract is identified and concludes when the RFP is released. In the following 10 steps I include information on how government issues Revisions, Modifications and Amendments (RMAs) to the solicitation. These are corrections and clarifications to the solicitation so potential bidders have a clear understanding of the most recent, revised requirements. Lastly, I'll offer an explanation of two government procurement timelines that may help your Business Development Manager anticipate government's Phase A process.

The process government uses to produce the RFP you are about to bid is a mystery at best. My objective in this chapter is to demystify this process by describing the inner workings of government so you can use this information to your competitive advantage. Specific benefits you will derive from this chapter include understanding: how a contract is designated as a small business set-aside, how government evaluates your Statement of Capabilities (SOC) so you can help influence a contract to become a set-aside, the importance of the Bidders' Conference, and procurement timelines. Procurement timelines will help you anticipate and plan for the government's next move, from identifying the requirement for a contract through contract award.

Later, in Chapter 5, Phase 1, Marketing to Government and Preparing to Receive the RFP, we will see how these Phase A government milestones dovetail with ongoing business development activities within your own company. Let's begin.

The 10 steps in Phase A are:

STEP 1: Identify Requirements
STEP 2: Develop Procurement "Design"
STEP 3: Conduct Market Analysis
STEP 4: Issue Sources Sought Synopsis
STEP 5: Evaluate Statement of Capabilities (SOC)
STEP 6: Issue Draft RFP
STEP 7: Conduct Bidders' Conference
STEP 8: Issue the RFP
STEP 9: Issue Revisions, Modifications, and Amendments (RMAs)
STEP 10: Establish Procurement Timelines

STEP 1: Identify Requirements

The government's process of developing a solicitation begins when something triggers the need for a contract. If this is a one-time procurement, an example might be an emerging need to develop a software control system to support test operations, where you can't necessarily anticipate a follow-on. If it's a recurring contract for a product or service and the existing contract is about to expire, the government processes a follow-on contract so there is continuity of this support. In other instances, the Contracting Office may recognize numerous re-procurements for products or services that are causing a manpower drain on their office. This routine need may result in a long-term contract, in lieu of individual Purchase Requisitions, or a multi-year contract in lieu of the year-by-year contract they've previously issued. As government moves to downsizing their Contracting Offices and transitioning to bundle contracts, changes such as these are commonplace.

STEP 2: Procurement Design

Procurement design results from discussions between the Contracts Office and user of the product or service on how best to package the solicitation for bid. This is done in close coordination with the SBS, who can help clarify if there are capable, qualified small businesses to perform the work. Procurement design consists of the duration of the contract—for example, a 3-year base contract with two, 1-year options for a total of 5-years, whether the contract should be a small business set-aside, the dollar value ceiling on the contract, and whether the contract award should be made based on low price or best value. The government PM will have the most current sense of the procurement design. The SBS will probably share new trends he or she is seeing from recent procurements. Basically, everything you read in the Sources Sought Synopsis is government's first best effort to design what will eventually become the solicitation you bid.

STEP 3: Market Analysis

As the name implies, Market Analysis (or Market Research as it's frequently called) is performed by the government to determine if there is adequate competition. These results can greatly influence the procurement design in STEP 2. If government anticipates very limited competition at the onset, this may be one of those unique instances where a contract could be awarded sole source to one company without competition. Be advised that when this occurs, government is still required to advertise its intent to award a sole source contract and to which company. This is your one opportunity to influence the decision by making it known that you can *also* deliver on all the contract requirements. Typically it's the government user of the product or service who best knows who might be interested in bidding. Government may also do research though the Internet or the Central Contractor Registry (CCR). It's possible to research the CCR by means of the North American Industry Classification (NAICS) or the Standard Industrial Codes

(SIC); or a keyword search. A common complaint I hear from SBSs that they frequently find information on the CCR that is out of date and therefore cannot contact the company's representative through an "old" phone number or email. Therefore, they cannot reach the company's point of contact to check if they are interested or even available to perform on the contract being researched. As I understand it, this occurs on about one in three occasions when the Contracting Office or PM performs small company research through the CCR. So it's advisable to update the CCR when there are changes in your company's contact information, NAICSs, company size, etc.

STEP 4: Issue Sources Sought Synopsis

When a solicitation is still in the formative stages the CO or CS will post a Sources Sought Synopsis on FedBizOpps (FBO). This is to identify companies that may be interested in bidding. Procurement actions of less than $25 k are not required to be posted on FBO and are typically handled by buyers through purchase requisitions or credit card purchases. The example posting for BRASS in Section 4.4.1, includes a brief statement of the services government is looking to buy and a point of contact, typically the CS. It is common for government to ask interested bidders to submit their Statement of Capabilities (SOC) so they can validate that the companies interested in bidding are capable and qualified of doing the work. If government identifies at least two companies within the same set-aside category, they are obliged to make it a set-aside contract.

4.4.1 Example Sources Sought Synopsis

The example Sources Sought Synopsis was taken directly from FedBizOpps. I omitted information like the last name, phone number and email for the CS assigned to this contract action. I inserted the *underlined* parts to highlight the details of the solicitation determined by the government through their Procurement Design described above in STEP 2. This information is indispensable to you. It can help you decide at this early stage not to bid and move onto a more promising opportunity. More importantly, if you do intend to bid, the underlined parts will help you begin addressing the long-lead actions that will help you position your company to WIN. I'll discuss this further in Phase 1, when I describe the activities going on in your company while government is developing the RFP in Phase A.

4.4.2 BRASS Sources Sought Synopsis Dated 8 June

> This effort is a <u>recompetition</u> of the existing Business and Staff Support (BASS) contract. The new effort is entitled <u>Business Resources and Support Services (BRASS)</u>. The scope of this effort is to acquire <u>business support, including all administrative support areas as referenced below, and program management</u> activities within the <u>Air Force Research Laboratory (AFRL), Directed Energy (DE) and Space Vehicle (VS) Directorates</u> located on <u>Kirtland AFB</u>, NM. The Government intends to award an indefinite-delivery, indefinite-quantity (ID/IQ) contract and issue <u>task orders (TOs)</u> - <u>Cost Plus Fixed Fee (CPFF)</u> or <u>Firm Fixed Price (FFP)</u> for an ordering period of 5 years with an anticipated maximum ordering <u>value of $49M</u>. Only <u>8(a) certified contractors</u> should respond to this notice by <u>submitting a Statement of Capability (SOC)</u>. Based upon the results of the SOC evaluation, the Government reserves the right to compete this effort as a competitive <u>8(a) set-aside</u>.

The underlined information in the BRASS Synopsis above will be used later when you make your decision to bid or no-bid the contract.

4.4.3 Why I Chose the BRASS RFP as the Example

I chose the Business Resources and Support Services (BRASS) RFP to explain the process of reviewing and responding to an RFP for the following reasons:

- BRASS is a recent, set-aside, but competitive contract – An important outcome of government's trend toward contract bundling.

- BRASS is an ID/IQ Contract that has its baseline Task (or Delivery) Order funded by the client Program Office's, whereby the balance of the funding comes from paying customers throughout government.

- BRASS is a performance-based professional services contract – it is indicative of a trend to outsource business functions historically performed by government employees.

- Past Performance is an important factor in determining who will WIN the award.

- Stringent Quality Requirements – An astute company develops its proposal sections and acknowledges the tightly-coupled interrelationship between Past Performance and Performance Measurements in the company's quality approach. If you tailor the measurements you are monitoring in your quality approach with the ones asked for in the RFP, you will save both time and money.

- Although the contract is for 5-years with no options, the contract's initial Task Orders will be issued for 2-years, which essentially gives the government the advantage of contract options. If your performance is not up to standards, government may choose to zero-fund the out years of your contract and subsequently release another solicitation for bid.

The relevance of BRASS as a good example in government contracting cannot be overstated. Outsourcing of government functions is a growth opportunity for any company that can deliver capable, qualified talent. In a recent live workshop, a representative from a small company prepared to bid on a re-compete (recurring) contract with the Department of State (DOS). I didn't know it at the time, but the typical DOS office has about 100 people—25 government personnel and the remaining 75 provided by contractor support through a multi-year contract. In fact, Professional and Administrative Service Contracts represent $122B, or 60 percent of all professional service contracts throughout government. Within this huge chunk of work is government outsourced IT Services ranked first as an outsourced support function, with an astounding 13 percent growth rate over the past 5 years. General professional services support grew at 11 percent per year during this same period. Therefore, as government cuts back on their civilian and military workforce, professional services contracts are becoming the preferred alternative.

STEP 5: Evaluate Statement of Capabilities (SOC)

After receiving your Statement of Capabilities, the government conducts a review of your submission. This review is subjective and not nearly as rigorous as the proposal evaluation that occurs later on; the government desires merely to validate which companies might bid in the future. Table 6 shows an example of how government summarizes their review of SOCs from four companies. In reviewing this table we see each contractor's SOC is reviewed for each requirement called out in the Sources Sought: proof of 8(a) status, expertise across several categories of labor, the need for security clearances, etc. The actual list is longer than that displayed in the example table, but this should provide you with a glimpse of how your SOC is evaluated. What is important is that each line evaluated is based on a requirement you read in the synopsis. This review confirmed the government's Market Analysis that there would in fact be sufficient competition within the contractor 8(a) set-aside community.

Table 6. Summary of How Your Statement of
Capabilities (SOC) Submission is
Evaluated

Evaluation of Capability Statements				
Summary of Topics Rated	**Contrac-tor #1**	**Contrac-tor #2**	**Contrac-tor #3**	**Contrac-tor #4**
(1) Proof of 8(a) status				
(2) Expertise in the areas of:				
Administrative Support				
Financial Management				
Program/Project Support				
Program Control Support				
SECRET Cleared Personnel				
(3) Demonstration of prior contract performance within last three years				

STEP 6: Issue Draft RFP

If you're fortunate to pursue an upcoming contract that has a Draft
RFP, it holds great value for both the government and for you. A
Draft RFP benefits the government through your feedback, which
can alleviate RMAs later on. For you, the benefit lies in having an
additional period of time to work on your proposal, especially the
long-lead items that I describe further in Chapter 6, STEP 8.
Although this book focuses on proposal writing for the small
business community, it should be noted that when a large
company—for example, a Boeing or a Lockheed Martin—
receives a Draft RFP it is not uncommon for about 60 percent of
the proposal to be essentially completed by the time the final RFP
is issued. This shifts the majority of the proposal creative process
to the period before the Final RFP is out, leaving most of that
precious 4, 6 or 8 week period for completing and refining an
already good proposal. The moral of the story is that if you happen

to have a Draft RFP issued, take advantage of it. I can assure you that other, more ambitious contractors will.

4.6.1 What is in a Solicitation?

A solicitation may take the form of an Invitation for Bid (IFB), Request for Quote (RFQ) or, in the case of BRASS, a Request for Proposal (RFP). The IFB is the simplest for of bid, next is the RFQ typically on Fixed-Price contracts. The RFP is the most complex solicitation and is most often applied to negotiated contracts. The FAR calls out the main sections of the RFP which government uses as a template to ensure the solicitation is complete before being released. This includes Sections A through M which are described in Figure 5.

Figure 5. Sections in a Typical RFP

Section A. Information to Offerors - Identifies the title of the procurement, procurement number, Point of Contact (POC), how to acknowledge amendments, and how to indicate "No Response" if you choose not to bid. Section A often appears as a 1-page form (Standard Form or SF33) that is signed by the contractor committing their company to the attached proposal (offer).

Section B. Supplies or Services and Price/Costs - This is where you provide your pricing. It defines the type of contract, the billable items or Contract Line Item Numbers (CLIN) that identify the contract, describes the period of performance, identifies option periods (if any), and provides cost and pricing guidelines. I frequently see labs providing a fill-in-the-blank table as an attachment to this section. For the bidder, it provides a template they can easily follow. For the lab, it eases their review during proposal evaluation.

Section C. Statement of Work (SOW) - Describes what the Government wants you to do or supply. Outside of your pricing, most of your proposal will be responding to this section. Here is where government tells you what to deliver. Lengthy Statements of Work (SOW) are typically referenced in this section and contained in their entirety as appendices in Section J. This is the case with BRASS where Section C is but one brief paragraph that refers you to the Performance Work Statements (PWS) in Section J.

Section D. Packages and Marking - Defines how all contract deliverables such as reports and material will be packaged and shipped. This may affect costs.

Section E. Inspection and Acceptance - Describes the process by which the government will officially accept deliverables and contractor procedures should the work not be accepted.

Section F. Deliveries or Performance - Defines how the Government Contracting Officer will control the work performed, and how you will deliver certain contract items. This section includes important information such as your day-to-day government POC on the contract. This person is most likely the COR.

Section G. Contract Administrative Data - Describes how the Government Contracting Officer and your firm will interact, and how information will be exchanged in administering the contract to ensure your performance and their prompt payment.

Section H. Special Contract Requirements - Contains a range of special contract requirements important to this particular procurement, such as procedures for managing changes to the original terms of the contract, government-furnished equipment (GFE) requirements, and government-furnished property (GFP) requirements. If there is a requirement for you to provide security-cleared personnel on the contract, here is where you will see it.

Section I. Contract Clauses/General Provisions - Identifies the contract clauses incorporated by reference in the RFP. These clauses will be incorporated into the contract. While it doesn't require a separate response, its terms will be binding if you are awarded the contract. I described three types of clauses you may encounter in Section 2.2 so you make the best use of your time when reading solicitation clauses.

Section J. Attachments and Exhibits - Lists the appendices to the RFP. These attachments can cover a wide range of subjects, from technical specifications through lists of GFE. It generally is used to provide data you need in order to respond to the SOW.

Section K. Representations/Certifications, and Statements of Offerors - Contains things that must be certified to bid on this contract. These can include things such as certification that the offeror has acted according to procurement integrity regulations, your taxpayer identification number, the status of personnel, ownership of your firm, type of business organization, authorized negotiators, compliance with affirmative action guidelines, and whether you qualify as a small business, disadvantaged business, and/or women-owned business. In BRASS, this is where you certify you're an 8(a) firm.

Section L. Proposal Preparation Instructions - Provides instructions for preparing the proposal. These include any formatting requirements, how the government wants your proposal organized, how to submit questions regarding the RFP or procurement, how the proposal is to be delivered, and other instructions.

Section M. Evaluation Criteria – This is an important section. It defines the factors used to "grade" your proposal. Proposals are graded, and costs are then considered to determine who wins the contract.

There are a few salient features of these sections you should be aware of. First, the majority of our time in this book will be spent on Sections C, L, and M, the SOW; Proposal Preparation Instructions; and Evaluation Criteria; respectively. These sections will help us create the detailed outline for our proposal in Chapter 9. Also, a Draft RFP may not include all of the sections described above. At a minimum you should expect the SOW and Evaluation Criteria. Oftentimes, Section M mimics much of what you read in Section L.

In Section A you may choose to let the government know that you do not intend to bid this particular solicitation. In Section E, it's prudent to include the time frame in which you will accept returns by the government. This is to prevent government from returning comments on a report 1 year after they received it where the people who created the report have since moved on to other projects. If you deliver hardware, this point is particularly important to ensure you don't have a warranty claim a year after your guarantee has expired simply because government didn't get around to opening the box and turning it on.

Section G lets you know if a Program Manager has been assigned to get this contract through award, or if it's being run out of the Contracts Office. Remember, it's much easier to get information from the Program Office than the Contracts Office, providing you ask your questions before Blackout.

In many parts of government and in the university-run national laboratories, the section headings and vocabulary are commonplace. Private company-run labs and some agencies of government are moving toward more commercial-style practices. In that case, the information embodied in the main sections A through M are still covered in the solicitations, but in a more abbreviated form with fewer pages and less likelihood of inconsistencies because of less redundancy. The commercial practices-type of solicitation is becoming more commonplace in the dreaded 2-week proposal I described in Section 2.8. Although government agencies and labs following commercial practices may not use these section headings, rest assured their solicitations will include a paragraph or section stating how your proposal will be evaluated (Evaluation Criteria, Section M), a description of what the organization wants SOW (Section C), your bid or cost to do the work (Section B: Price/Costs), etc.

STEP 7: Conduct Bidders' Conference

The government's objective in conducting a Bidders' Conference is to level the playing field. Sometimes the conference is called the Pre-Proposal Conference or Industry Day. Regardless of what the forum is called, the playing field is leveled by providing information, and possibly facility tours, to ensure all participants feel they have a sufficient understanding of the requirements to decide to bid and write their proposals. Bidders' Conferences are especially important on recurring contracts where potential bidders feel the incumbent has an unfair advantage. It can also be a useful tool to convey how the client's organization is run and how work on the contract is performed. A big advantage to you is the opportunity to see first hand the facilities and environment your people would work in if you win the contract. Feedback to the government during and after the Bidders' Conference is probably your last opportunity to influence the language in the solicitation. Also, it's a great opportunity to team with others. I can recall one recent Bidders' Conference where the winner found two of their three subcontractors at this forum. These Bidders' Conferences include government presentations where you may also meet the contract PM (future COR), SSA, CO, and CS.

STEP 8: Issue the RFP

At this point the complete solicitation, including all of the sections described in Section 4.6.1, is distributed to anyone who may choose to bid. This is now routinely and conveniently done by downloading PDF or Word files from FedBizOpps.

STEP 9: Issue Revisions, Modifications and Amendments (RMAs)

The government issues changes to a solicitation through FedBizOpps as Revisions, Modifications or Amendments (RMAs). Some changes can be small while others can be quite involved. In isolated instances, the number or content of the revisions may merit the government reissuing the entire solicitation. The more complex the RFP, the more likely there will be changes made after the RFP is released. Many of these revisions can be avoided by issuing a Draft RFP. However, government exercises their discretion in this matter.

STEP 10: Procurement Timelines

One important function of the Business Development Manager (BDM) is to plan company milestones to better position the company to bid. To accomplish this, the BDM must have an idea of how long the government's process takes. Table 8 includes two example procurement timelines that can be used to plan for your next opportunity. This is the kind of timeline used by government's procurement PM to ensure the contract is awarded on time. The "short timeline" is associated with what some agencies call streamlined procurement or fast-track procurement. Regardless of what it's called, this procurement provides a speedier processing time from inception to contract award. The threshold of what constitutes a fast-track procurement is frequently based on a dollar threshold. The dollar threshold for a fast-track procurement may be $1 million in one agency while it could be $50 million at another. Once you understand the dollar threshold that constitutes a typical procurement timeline for the organization you are working with, you can plan for the milestones that are important to you.

Table 7. Procurement Timelines

Contract Milestone	Short Time (months)	Typical Timelines (months)
Develop Requirements	-7.0	-17.5
Sources Sought Advertised	-5.0	-11.5
Draft RFP Released	-4.5	-7.5
Bidders' Conference	-4.0	-7.0
Issue RFP	-2.0	-5.0
Proposals Due	-1.0	-4.0
Contract Award	0.0	0.0
Start Work	+0.25	+0.25
Phase-in Complete	+1.25	+1.25

As you can see, a short procurement timeline for the federal government or a lab can begin 7 months before contract award. This timeline can stretch to almost 1.5 years for a typical procurement. Also, the duration; from receipt of proposal to contract award can range from 1 month to 4 months in the examples in Table 8.

4.10.1 BRASS Procurement Timeline

The procurement timelines described in Table 8 were rules of thumb for planning purposes. Let's look at the BRASS procurement as an actual example. We can see in Figure 6 the various procurement milestones published in FedBizOpps; these are not estimates. Note that the government issued a Sources Sought Synopsis on June 8. The PM and Contracting Office were working on this procurement probably months before the Sources Sought was published in FedBizOpps. Interested companies had until July 5 (1 month) to submit their SOCs showing that they were possibly interested in bidding. About 2 weeks later, on July 20, government published a list of the companies that submitted SOCs. I can only surmise this list was intended to replace the Bidders' Conference, which does not show up on this timeline. Draft Performance Work Statement's (PWSs) were issued September 2, and on October 25 a Draft RFP, or an expansion of the September PWSs, was issued. On November 18, the final RFP was issued, just in time for the holidays. A revision and an amendment to the solicitation were issued, and contractor questions and government's answers published.

We see that proposals were due January 17 of the following year, so bidders had about 8 weeks to prepare their proposals. I frequently see 6-week proposal times for R&D contracts, but rarely see 8 weeks. In summary, the trained eye should notice the unusually long period to bid and when there is no Bidders' Conference, you can probably estimate about 4 months for the government to award the contract after proposals are received. So, as you can see, the total lapsed time from the advertisement of Sources Sought through contract award was about a full year. But the government started working this procurement action long before issuing the Sources Sought Synopsis, and government may in fact take as much as 6 months from receipt of proposals to award. The 6 months, 180 days, was cited in Block 12 of the Standard Form (SF33) where government asked your bids be "good" for that long. So, as you can see, this entire process can easily take 15 to 18 months. This long lead time should prompt the BDM to begin asking questions of the government PM, CO, or CS long before the Synopsis is posted on FedBizOpps.

Figure 6. BRASS Procurement Timeline

June	July	August	September	October	November	December	January		
▲ 8 Jun: Sources Sought Synopsis									
	▲ 5 Jul: Statement of Capability Submissions Due								
	▲ 20 Jul: 8a Vendor List								
			▲ 2 Sep: DRAFT Performance Work Statement (PWS) 01						
				▲ 25 Oct: Notice of Contract Action 01 (DRAFT RFP)					
					▲ 18 Nov: DD Form 1707 Information to Offerors				
					▲ 18 Nov: RFP with Attachments 01				
					▲ 29 Nov: Revised Cost Proposal Instructions				
						▲ 1 Dec: Amendment 01 1 Dec: Q & A #1			
						▲ 9 Dec: Amendment 02			
						▲ 19 Dec Q&A #2			
							▲ 1 Jan Q&A #3		
							▲ 5 Jan Q&A #4		
							▲ 17 Jan: Proposals Due		

Chapter 5.0 Marketing to Government and Preparing to Receive the RFP (Phase 1)

This chapter describes the activities within your company to identify business opportunities, gather information, decide whether to bid, and position your company to compete for a contract. This work is primarily the responsibility of the BDM with a handoff to the proposal manager if it appears you will bid. The Five-Phase Approach™ in Figure 4, in Section 3.4, shows Phase 1 occurring in parallel with government's development of the RFP in Phase A. This occurs when you are looking at a snapshot of one solicitation that is being developed by government and you're tracking that procurement. In reality, your Phase 1 is an ongoing process by the BDM to identify opportunities to possibly bid and pare down to the chosen few contracts you will actually bid. So Phase 1 for a single solicitation occurs before receiving the RFP. Below is a list of the 12 steps that occur in Phase 1. Steps 1 through 3 will be discussed in this chapter and Steps 4 through 12 will be covered in Chapter 6.

STEP 1: Develop Strategic Plan
STEP 2: Identify Business Opportunities
STEP 3: Gather Intelligence
STEP 4: Tailor Statement of Capabilities (SOC)
STEP 5: Review Draft RFP
STEP 6: Make Bid/No-Bid Decision
STEP 7: Form Draft Proposal Team

STEP 1: Develop Strategic Plan

Successful business development strategy and, hence, successful proposals are not merely written. They are developed as an integral part of a lengthy planning process that begins with strategic planning. There are hundreds of strategic planning models. I'll use one approach to introduce this topic and then explain the important relationship between strategic planning and business development.

Every company must have a purpose, a reason to exist. This is their *mission*. Routinely, when thinking about your company's future, you may sketch a picture of this future company that doesn't exactly coincide with its present product or service mix or position within their industry. That's OK. That's your corporate *Vision*—a statement of where you want your company to be in the future. It's the vital link between your mission and your vision that forms your strategic plan. It's the road map that guides your company toward that new company that presently exists only in your mind.

Figure 7 shows the evolution of a corporate mission and vision into the follow-on actions that become your strategic plan. The gap between your mission and vision is translated into goals, objectives, actionable tasks and, lastly, a means to measure progress in the plan's implementation. An analysis of Strengths, Weaknesses, Opportunities, and Threats (SWOT) is an input and influences your vision and the direction you wish to take your company. The strategic plan is developed by the company executive and functional managers. These managers may represent Marketing or Business Development, Human Resources, Operations, etc.

Figure 7. Corporate Strategic Planning Model

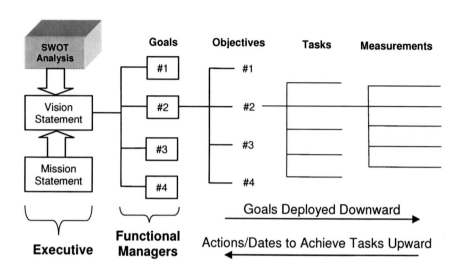

One example of a goal is to diversify into the public sector, specifically the federal government market. Actionable objectives that support this goal may include "secure first federal government contract in Year 2 (Objective 1)" and "25 percent of company revenues will come from federal contracts by Year 5 (Objective 2)."

To achieve Objective 1, secure first federal government contract in Year 2, "tasks must be planned and executed. Actionable tasks may include assess government business prospects within a 4-hour commute of our corporate offices by searching their web sites and having initial discussions with their SBS and register and with the SBA, PTAC, and local agencies so you are notified of upcoming small business conferences and training; assess the need to hire a government marketing specialist to develop the federal market or groom in-house talent.

Lastly, the successful execution tasks need a planned completion date to assess local business prospects and review their web sites summarizing the specific names of agency Points of Contact (POC) each Pocks name, title, area of responsibility, contract authority amount, best contact information, the local small business forums he supports, etc. Although these tasks may be performed by your BDM or Subject SMEs, progress will be regularly assessed by the executive and functional managers to ensure specific actions are being taken to move the company down a proactive path of diversification within the 2-5-year milestones documented in their strategic plan.

You may be asking, "Gee, do we really need to have a strategic plan to secure government business?" The answer is a resounding, "Yes!" The benefit of having a strategic plan is to help company management allocate scarce resources to pursue the most promising new initiatives. Eventually, every discussion to approve one initiative over another rests on the promise of their results, their costs to implement, and the company's priorities. The presence of a strategic plan is the tie breaker in such discussions. Furthermore, when trying to decide which contract to bid and which one to let pass by, having a clear understanding of your direction and priorities makes these decisions much easier.

You've removed most of the road-blocks to success when you've learnt the difference between motion and direction.

Bill Copeland

5.1.1 SWOT Analysis

A SWOT analysis is a facilitated exercise, as is strategic planning. A facilitator begins by drawing and labeling the following table on a flip-chart. Everyone in the meeting is asked to identify SWOTs, starting with one person and then proceeding around the room.

Table 8. SWOT Exercise

Strengths	Weaknesses
Opportunities	Threats

Audience inputs may begin taking shape as follows.

Strengths

- Our company has a loyal following in the private sector in two industries: _____ and _____.
- Our employees are loyal and our retention rate is better than our competitors.
- We enjoy a reputation for delivering high-quality delivery performance.
- We possess a unique rapid response capability.
- We have multiple industry experience.
- We are very client oriented.

Weaknesses

- We haven't implemented online ordering. This seems to be a trend where we're viewed as a follower, not a leader.
- We're short in some skill sets seen in recent solicitations.

Opportunities

- Local agencies of the federal government are transitioning to multi-year contracts to buy our services. In the past, individual PRs did not make it attractive enough to pursue government business.

Threats

- We're experiencing the beginning indications of a recession in our private sector clients. This may be an opportune time to pursue government contracts for workload leveling.

- A new local competitor has lured away two of our long-term clients through lower pricing.

- Regional, not only local competing companies, are courting our clients through advances in technology.

Although this is an abbreviated version of what would be gleaned from a SWOT Analysis spanning 1 or 2 days, you can see a picture forming to compel company leadership to begin considering a new direction. The need to replace private-sector business due to a decline in the economy, the necessity to e-commerce online ordering, and the promise of long-term government contracts are but a few. Much of this information will be used when developing your proposal theme in Chapter 7. The Proposal Strategy may result in tasks that will help pre-position your company to better compete for future contracts. This too will be described in Chapter 7.

STEP 2: Identify Business Opportunities

Step 2 will help you identify business opportunities and uncover information that will help you understand the inner workings of the client's organization. As in any marketing effort, there are many ways to identify contract opportunities. You will determine over time which source works best for you. Some sources are listed below.

- FedBizOpps
- National Laboratories websites
- Organization research
- Annual, general events
- Professional associations
- Contract-specific events

5.2.1 Federal Business Opportunities (FedBizOpps)

The web site—www.FedBizOpps.gov (or FBO)—is the federal government's single source for all contracts over $25k in value. You can search the database by the commodity or service you offer, by NAIC code, by agency of government or by geographic location. An example of a FBO web page is included in Figure 8. These are the postings on FBO for the BRASS contract I have been using as my example. Each entry takes you to the specifics for that posting by simply clicking on that link. Note the first posting includes a Sources Sought Synopsis; often this may be the first time you become aware of the solicitation. The next posting is a list of 8(a) vendors who were interested enough in the contract to submit a SOC. This list can help you identify potential teaming partners. Next is a Draft Performance Work Statement (PWS) wherein government gives you insights into the details of at least one PWS they intend to include in the final release of the solicitation. Be advised, in this case government is only issuing a Draft PWS. On other contracts, this posting may include other information such as Proposal Evaluation Criteria (Section M) or Instructions to the Contractor (Section L). In other instances government may choose to provide you with a Draft of the entire procurement package, Sections A through M. Amendments 01 and 02 are posted to reflect small changes in the solicitation. There are also two postings for contractor questions and the government's response. At the bottom of Figure 8, I made a note that proposals are due January 17. If I had waited until this contract was awarded, you would also see a posting announcing the winner of the contract and the dollar value of the award.

Figure 8. FedBizOpps Postings for BRASS Contract Announcements

Synopsis - Posted on Jun 08

8(a) Vendor List for Sources Sought Synopsis 01 - Posted on Jul 20

Draft Performance Work Statement 01 - Posted on Sep 09

Notice of Contract Action 01 - Posted on Oct 25

DD Form 1707 - Information to Offerors or Quoters Section A Cover Sheet 01 - Posted on Nov 18

BRASS RFP with Attachments 01 - Posted on Nov 18

Revise Cost Proposal Instructions - Use these instructions vs Atch 28 - 01 - Posted on Nov 29

Amendment 01 - Posted on Dec 01

Questions/Answers to RFP FA9451-05-R-0003 01 - Posted on Dec 01

Amendment 02 - Posted on Dec 09

#2 SET OF QUESTIONS/ANSWERS FA9451-05-R-0003 BRASS 01 - Posted on Dec 19

Solicitation Number: FA9451-05-R-0003   Title: R -- Professional, Administrative, and Management Support Services

5.2.2 National Laboratory Websites

National laboratories typically post contract opportunities on their websites. It's unusual to see them use FBO. In fact, if you do see a lab posting on FBO, it's an indication they're having difficulty rallying sufficient competition through their own in-house sources. You can find links to the DOEs 21 laboratories and technology centers by clinking on the link below.

http://www.energy.gov/organization/labs-techcenters.htm

One lab you'll find at this website is Lawrence Berkeley National Laboratory. Lawrence Berkeley is located in the hills above the University of California's Berkeley campus, adjacent to the San Francisco Bay. They're managed by the University of California and conduct unclassified research across a wide range of scientific disciplines including fundamental studies of the universe, quantitative biology, nanoscience; new energy systems, and the environment. These technical terms may help you decide if you can support one or more core functions in any of their seventeen scientific divisions. If your products and services support Small City-type contracts, you'll find Berkeley's 200 acre, 3,800-employee campus to be fertile ground for contracts that any large company, military base, or laboratory campus might use. If you go to their website you can click on their Forecasted Contracting Opportunities. Table 9 displays a small portion of the upcoming contract opportunities at Berkeley. Be reminded, while government and the labs are continuing to do a much better job of forecasting contracting opportunities, such resources still primarily include Small City, recurring contracts that are easy to predict.

Table 9. Berkeley Laboratory Forecasted Contracting Opportunities (Excerpt)

NAICS Code	Description	Estimated Value / Solicitation Method	Solicitation Release Date / Expected Award Date
541330	Engineering / Construction Test Services	$100K - $500 Small Business Set-Aside	FY06 - 3rd qtr. FY06 - 3rd qtr.
561710	Pest Control Services	$25K - $50K SB Set-Aside	FY06 - 3rd qtr. FY06 - 3rd qtr.
TBD	Seismic Retrofit - Bldg. 50 & 74	$1M - $5M Full / Open	FY06 - 4th qtr. FY06 - 4th qtr.
562111 562920 423930	Waste Handling Removal / Recycling	$100K - $500K Full / Open	FY06 - 4th qtr. FY06 - 4th qtr.
424690	Industrial Gases	$250K + TBD	FY06 - 4th qtr. FY07 - 1st qtr.
421430	IT Networking Equipment	$500K - $900K TBD	FY07 - 1st qtr. FY07 - 4th qtr.

5.2.3 Research Organization

If you search FedBizOpps (FBO) to identify which agencies of government use your product or service you may notice almost every agency uses what you sell. This is especially true of those businesses that support Small City contracts. If your business supports core functions, your list of opportunities may be shorter, but you have the advantage of funding, contracts and priorities that are managed by a PO who is open to providing the information you need in making your decision to bid. There are advantages to both kinds of contracts, and in either case, you will find the Federal Aviation Administration (FAA), Social Security Agency (SSA), Forest Service, and any number of other agencies who also use what you sell. The first place to look for products and services government buys can be easily found on their website.

Your next task will be to learn more about the organization offering the contract and verify that they do buy what you sell. This is done by reviewing their website. All government agencies and labs have buttons on their websites with labels like: "what we buy;" "how to do business with us;" "the procurement office;" "the small business office;" "how we are organized;" and so forth. Your brief review of their site will confirm what they buy and who might be a good first point of contact to introduce yourself to the organization.

There are notable exceptions though. I recently spoke with a woman who offered soft-skills training: leadership, communication, teambuilding, etc. The nearby national lab did not advertise those kinds of contracts on their website. In this case, a brief conversation with the Human Resources Department who contracted for training was the appropriate contact. This was discovered through a referral by the SBS.

Further research, either on the web, over the telephone, or by email, should answer your additional questions regarding how often they buy, which type of contract vehicle they use to buy, the dollar value of a typical contract, and other specifics of how actively they're bundling contracts, whether they are using past performance as a factor in contract awards, etc. For a BDM desiring to identify contract opportunities over the next few years, an organization's website, followed by a few questions to the Small Business Office, the Contracting Office, or, in the case of core functions, to the requisite Program Office, will allow you to quickly "qualify" a prospect. Also, all labs publish a list of what has been spent on each contract. This is done annually. Although you may have been notified of the contract value shortly after contract award, this document sheds light on what is actually being spent.

5.2.4 Annual, General Events

It's common for agencies of government and national labs to host events on a community, state, or regional basis to help small businesses connect with upcoming contract opportunities. Once you begin networking and registering with these organizations you will be notified of such events. These forums typically include presentations on how to do business with the agency or lab, as well as upcoming contract opportunities and trainings on specific topics designed to assist small companies. I have presented 1 hour overviews of my Five-Phase Approach™ at such events. Other topics I have seen include registering on CCR, marketing to government, how to prepare a great Statement of Capabilities; how to process an electronic invoice for payment. Many of these forums also schedule time for you to meet one on one with a representative from the specific agency, lab or prime contractor you may be interested in courting. This one-on-one meeting provides you anywhere from 15 to 30 minutes of uninterrupted time to better understand their organization and identify specific people you might introduce to your product or service. Sometimes these forums are tailored for a set-aside category of small business such as Small Disadvantaged Business, 8(a), Woman-Owned, Veteran-Owned, Native American or a host of other set-aside categories. It has been my experience that, although you may not be a veteran, for example, or represent a small woman-owned business, you're still welcome to attend any of these forums.

My home state, New Mexico, has a great professional association called Professional Aerospace Contractors Association (PACA). Its purpose is to facilitate communication between government and the contractor community through monthly luncheons and an annual event in August. In their annual event, PACA specifies a format for government presenters to use to summarize upcoming contract opportunities. That format includes: the title of the procurement action, anticipated date of RFP release, anticipated contract award, estimated contract value and government point of contact. Like my lab example in Table 9, the PACA annual event provides a wealth of invaluable information for any business development professional. From this one event, you could map out upcoming bid opportunities for the next 1 or 2 years, identify teaming opportunities and initiate networking relationships that will last throughout your entire career. Unlike the Berkeley Lab example I used earlier, these presentations include not only recurring contracts, but developmental and one-time procurement actions. Because the government and lab marketplace has such a huge R&D presence, these contracts focus on specific research efforts and also include BAAs and SBIRs to identify promising contract opportunities that may lead to research with universities and/or a future commercial product. You probably have a similar association by another name in your area such as Southern California Aerospace Professionals (SCAPR) in El Segundo, CA.

Another resource that hosts state, regional and national business development events is the National Defense Industrial Association (NDIA). A quick review of its website will uncover possible nearby events in your company's area of interest. Websites for both PACA and NDIA are included below.

PACA Website: http://www.pacanm.org/
NDIA Website: http://www.ndia.org/

5.2.5 Professional Associations

I cited PACA and the NDIA as a great way to identify business opportunities and develop partnering relations with other prime and subcontractors, but there are others. If you're involved in contracts in your company as a Contract Specialist, budget person or Proposal Manager, the National Contract Management Association (NCMA) is a fantastic resource for training and networking with peers in industry and in government. There's something disarming about sharing a meal during one of these events, strategically positioning yourself to sit beside the CO for the agency you're looking to do business with. This is a unique opportunity to understand how they do business and what kind of contract vehicles they use to buy what you sell. It's also a great opportunity to learn about upcoming changes in the way they do business, how new policies will impact your business or to find out how they do contract bundling. That knowledge can shorten the time you will need to prepare for your next proposal.

If you deliver construction or Architectural and Engineering (A&E) services it's imperative for you to belong to the Society of Military Engineers (SME), particularly if you do projects managed by the Army Corps of Engineers. Here, the person you're networking with could turn out to be the very CS who will assemble your next solicitation, or the PM who is developing requirements for an upcoming contract they will eventually be responsible for evaluating and managing. Other professional associations, depending on your specialty, include the International Test & Evaluation Association (ITEA), Directed Energy Professional Association (DEPA) and Association of Old Crows (AOC) if you're in the Electronic Warfare business. An association that can prove helpful across many industries is the Project Management Institute (PMI). With so many RFPs now asking for "certified" Project Managers, this association provides ready access to certified professionals as well as a rigorous training certification program that is widely recognized.

If you primarily support core functions, there are undoubtedly professional and trade associations that can provide networking opportunities and training. I'm most familiar with pulsed power and engineering associations that support our local core functions, but there are many others based on your specialty.

5.2.6 Contract-Specific Events

Sometimes referred to as a Bidders' Conference or Industry Day, these events are focused on presenting the details of an upcoming procurement action to would-be bidders. The intent of this forum is to foster competition and level the playing field. Leveling the playing field is especially important if it's a recurring contract where an incumbent is executing the existing contract. As at the general, annual events, this forum offers a unique opportunity to meet and network with government and potential contractor teaming partners. Unlike the general event discussed above, this event is focused on a specific contract where RFP release is imminent. In fact, you may have received a Draft RFP to review in advance of the Bidders' Conference to help you better prepare for this meeting and provide feedback to government. An important advantage of this event is that, because Final RFP release is imminent, it becomes urgent for companies to team up. During one recent procurement, later awarded to Honeywell, the company found two of their three subcontracts at the Bidders' Conference. Both the subs delivered specialized services that fit nicely into Honeywell's Small Business Plan accompanying their proposal.

5.2.7 Classify Opportunities

Often, company SMEs are so enamored with their technology they often forget the business side of business development. Therefore I have three priority levels for classifying opportunities. You can make the best use of your valuable time pursuing the most promising of those opportunities. They are

- Priority 1: Client has a budget
- Priority 2: Client may have SOW and/or schedule but no budget
- Priority 3: Client has a vision only

A *Priority 1* client has a budget and probably needs to award their contract by the end of the fiscal year, September 30. The earlier you discuss the details of the procurement before a Draft RFP is released, the freer a PM will be with information. You should routinely discuss upcoming opportunities with a Priority 1 client. This will build a good relationship and give you unique insights into the details of how they do business, which can help you plan your business future. You may even be asked to provide input describing the nature of the work that needs to be performed. If asked, this is a unique opportunity to provide information that eventually may become the SOW, list of deliverables, and budget estimate.

A *Priority 2* client with everything they need: SOW, list of deliverables, etc., but short of a budget may be ready to go to procurement. If the value of the procurement falls with the levels of monies, which are routinely reshuffled at the end of the fiscal year, an aggressive government PM may simply be waiting his or her turn for end-of-year fallout money. September 30 is the end of the fiscal year in the federal government and "fallout" money starts showing up about June. Depending on the agency you are working with, the dollar value for some of these end-of-year reshuffles can be in the 10's or 100's of thousands of dollars range. Priority 1 and Priority 2 clients require frequent visits, and good ideas may translate into procurement actions and subsequent awards.

A *Priority 3* client qualifies for less frequent contact. An ambitious government PM who has a track record for selling ideas and translating their plans into reality is probably in the conceptual stages of a possible contract. They are not positioned with a SOW in hand to take advantage of last minute contract opportunities and are probably waiting for next year or out year funding. Budget your time accordingly.

STEP 3: Gather Intelligence

Once you've opened up channels of information to help you understand how a potential client does business and how to successfully uncover opportunities, it's necessary to seek additional information to position your company to bid. This information will help you make an informed Bid/No-Bid Decision.

Now let's review sources to help you make decisions and conduct research. In this step I will describe six sources:

- Networking with Clients

- FedBizOpps

- Internet

- Freedom of Information Act (FOIA)

- Job Opening Advertisements

- Hire Critical Skills

5.3.1 Networking with Clients

Let us not overlook the most obvious source of information—networking. You can obtain valuable information from routine conversations with the Contracts Office, people in the Program Office and of course teaming partners. While the small business forums I mentioned above serve as a great place to start, it has been my experience that forums outside the particular bidding environment are far superior to help network and obtain valuable information. I mentioned earlier that it is much easier to obtain information from Program Office people such as project managers, project officers and the like. The barriers really come down in professional and trade association forums, facilitating communication with other professionals, especially if it gives you the opportunity to chat face-to-face. These contacts can provide you with intelligence on the performance of existing contractors, either on the contract you hope to bid or on similar work. A routine conversation with a user of that service, COR or PM, can give you information as to the importance of higher skill levels for technical personnel or past problem areas. Some may become theme points you may include in your bid, particularly if you can *ghost* the incumbent. *Ghosting* is the process where you exploit the incumbent's weaknesses, which coincidentally may be your strengths. Remember, despite all the barriers posed by rules, regulations, and FAR clauses, selling to government, like all selling, is still a people-to-people transaction. If someone in government is pleased or displeased with the work he's getting, he is sure to let you know. When asking a COR for advice on how to bid the next contract, if he or she says, "Gee, we'd give anything to have a contractor who can deliver reports on time," this might imply a weakness of the incumbent, and become a proposal theme point for you.

You can familiarize yourself with the incumbent's performance through one-on-one conversations with the government. This can provide invaluable insights into the strengths and weaknesses of the incumbent. This kind of information is easily obtained through people in the Program Office. At this stage you can also ask, "Who do you expect will bid this contract?" Communication with the government is pretty open until the Draft RFP is released. Contracts like BRASS present a unique opportunity to obtain valuable information. In this case the contract may be run out of the Contracting Office, but the contract supports people in the Program Office. So you're able to speak with both to form a more rounded picture of the incumbents' performance.

In the earlier part of Phase 1 you may persuade the client to modify the SOW or change the evaluation criteria to benefit both your company and the client. If the client has historically awarded fixed fee contracts, you may persuade them to look more broadly at the total life-cycle cost of the project, which might be better served by a best value award, offering reduced costs over the long term. If the client has historically awarded Cost Plus Fixed Fee Contracts, which do not play to your strengths, you may speak with the PM and CO to find out whether their decision is final.

5.3.2 FedBizOpps as a Data Mining Tool

As we described in Section 5.2.1 above, FBO is a great resource for identifying upcoming bid opportunities. Moreover, if you're a new company or new to doing business with a particular agency, a frequently asked question is, "Must I bid and lose several contracts before winning?" The answer is a resounding "No." A great way to accelerate your learning curve is to learn the operating rules for that organization. One way to increase your chances of WINning is to do some homework before receiving the RFP you're really interested in through *data mining.*

Through data mining you may use FBO to research past RFPs that \have already been awarded. They're typically posted for up to a year. This historical accounting of the RFP from posting of the Sources Sought Synopsis through Contract Award provides a wealth of information. First of all, it answers the big question, "How long does it take that organization to get a contract out?" While there is great variability in this process you can count the months it actually took to award a contract. You can also compare the contract dollar value against the SOW. The historical solicitation also gives you insights into the section and volumes the client typically requires, as well as page count and formatting requirements. This is a time saver that enables you to create templates for the contents of your proposal visuals in advance of the Final RFP being released. It also tells you whether that agency gives bidders 6 weeks, 4, or maybe just 2 weeks to bid. Armed with this information you can prepare in advance, and even start integrating sections of your proposal before the next RFP is posted. This approach is especially effective if you're in an industry that is typically given just a couple of weeks to bid.

5.3.3 The Internet

An Internet search can offer valuable insights into the inner workings of your competitors. Their websites can be a treasure-trove, revealing what they consider to be their strengths, as well as new developments in their company, that may give them a competitive edge on future contracts. We are all familiar with Google searches. When I researched BRASS I knew these kinds of professional services contracts were common. So I did a Google search on the character string A&AS—Advisory & Assistance Services. I uncovered a PowerPoint presentation delivered by the Air Force Colonel at Los Angeles Air Force Station who is the PM on an A&AS contract there. The briefing showed flow charts and narrative on how requirements become new R&D efforts and contractor task orders. It described the process in detail; the hand-offs between contractor and government and decision points. If I were bidding BRASS and had limited access to the internal workings of the organization offering the contract, this information would provide some visibility into the entire process. In any case, it would help me understand the business processes and ask clarifying questions of the client to help tailor my proposal.

The disadvantage of the Google search is that you often get too many hits that overwhelm you with the sheer volume of information. One tool I use is *Google Alert*, a free service, which allows you to enter the names of key employees on a competitor's staff, the company name or a string of key words. Google Alert will then search for specific topics that are currently being released through the open literature. Finally Google Alert notifies me of any publicly released information using the key works I specified.

One Internet resource available through the government to help match prime and subcontractors is Pro-Net. Pro-Net is a handy tool for large companies to perform searches for possible teaming partners to support upcoming procurement actions. In January 2004 Pro-Net's search capability and functions were integrated with CCR. This resource is not limited to private sector companies and may also include government and universities.

5.3.4 The Freedom of Information Act (FOIA)

The Freedom of Information Act is a useful tool for obtaining copies of government information. You may use the FOIA to find out about existing government contracts. At a minimum, the information provided will include the solicitation used on the existing contract, contract-funded reports and possibly even contractor invoices and billing rates. This information is especially valuable when you don't anticipate a Draft RFP. Although the existing solicitation may be years old, I can assure you that it probably did not change very much except for a few new requirements, either in the technical aspect or boiler plate contract clauses the government adds on. You can literally ask for the entire contract file on an incumbent. That's the good news.

The not-so-good news is that it can take several months to obtain this information, depending upon how willing the Contracting Office is to release the information. The CO may also delete information they consider to be sensitive or proprietary. A good rule of thumb is that the earlier in the procurement process you ask the client for this kind of information, the easier it is for the CS to simply make you a copy. An astute CS may simply reproduce the information if he knows a FOIA is going to be your next step, because saves the CS from having to deal with the suspense and headquarters follow-up that inevitably accompanies FOIA tracking. As you draw nearer to Blackout, the Contracting Office becomes very sensitive about any information related to the procurement and is reluctant to give it up.

5.3.5 Job Opening Advertisements

Job opening advertisements provide a good barometer reading of how people in the incumbent's company feel they will fare when the new contract is re-bid. Near my home, Kirtland Air Force Base has a base newspaper that frequently includes sizeable ads for companies collecting resumes in preparation for an upcoming bid. A deluge of resumes from the incumbent can give you insights into the vocabulary used on that contract as well as an indication that employees are ready for a change. This is so for any number of reasons. If the resumes are from more senior people, that serves as a clear indication that there is trouble in paradise and their present company is in jeopardy of losing the follow-on contract. This is also a valuable source of incumbent information through the interviewing process.

For the small company looking to grow dramatically with award of "that next contract," Job Search Agencies can provide a valuable service. Yes, they do charge a fee, but it is small in comparison with what it costs to create and maintain a Human Resources Department that is not continuously hiring.

5.3.6 Hire Critical Skills

Staffing up for a new contract is often a challenge. Where do you find the people who have the requisite skills, security clearances, and ability to work with others under less-than-ideal circumstances? The top people on your contract organizational chart are ,typically staffed through networking, professional associations and head hunters. But the working level and middle management, who make up the bulk of your workforce, can be found through a *Career Transition Office* at your local military installation. They maintain a database of men and woman who are either retiring or leaving the military after their tour and can be searched according to the skills or region of the country in which they wish to live and work. When a 30-person training company in Colorado Springs needed 60 people to support a training contract at Ft. Carson Army Base to teach refresher skills to soldiers about to be deployed to the war zone, they found their trainers through a database search of people with the combat training and requisite skills who were about to leave the military after a recent tour in a war zone. How better to train people about to go into harm's way?

Chapter 6.0 Marketing to Government (Phase 1 Cont.)

STEP 4: Tailor Statement of Capabilities

Every company has a document they regularly use to advertise their capabilities to prospective customers. There should be at least two versions of this SOC; the general and the tailored. You should freely pass out the general SOC to people you are meeting for the first time to broadly introduce the products and services you offer. It should be general enough so a potential client could say, "Tell me more about this," or "We can surely use that." It answers whether you can offer something they may need and sparks further conversation.

You also have an opportunity to submit a SOC in response to a Sources Sought Synopsis. This SOC should be tailored. It should be tailored in accordance with what the government is asking for in the Synopsis. This makes it easier for government to conclude you are capable and qualified to do the work. This is a key factor in their decision to make the contract a set-aside. In fact, if government can uncover two or more companies within any set-aside category, they are required to make it a set-aside contract. Therefore, nothing you do in advance of an RFP release does more to influence the level of competition in an upcoming contract than producing a well-written, tailored SOC. My web site, www.proposalw.com, has a FREE Download of what factors constitute a good SOC and a poor SOC.

Table 6, in Chapter 4, demonstrates how your SOC is evaluated by government. In the case of the BRASS Synopsis, I have prepared a list of requirements which follows the order requirements were described in the Synopsis. It also follows the order in which government will be checking off your response to each requirement. Because we now understand how government uses this information, the list below in Table 10 can be used as a template to tailor your SOC. On the left is the requirement. On the right would be your brief reply to each requirement.

Table 10. Organizing a Reply to Sources Sought Synopsis

Summary of Rated Topics	Your Company Reply to Requirement
(1) Proof of 8(a) status	
(2) Expertise in the areas of Support	
Administrative Support	
Financial Management	
Program/Project Support	
Other requirements	
(3) Demonstration of prior contract performance within last three years	

Note: This is a partial list of requirements for illustrative purposes.

STEP 5: Review Draft RFP

If you enjoy the opportunity of being issued a Draft RFP take advantage of it. The government will only issue a Draft RFP to help take an already good solicitation final. This minimizes the number of revisions, modifications and amendments later. For you, the Draft is an important tool to help you decide early on if you intend to bid. For example, reviewing companies on the distribution list will help you assess the competition which may influence your decision. To fully determine if you intend to bid, read the solicitation from cover to cover.

Draft RFP's take many forms. In some instances it includes Section A, the cover sheet or SF33, through M, Evaluation Criteria. Most often it contains only selected sections. At a minimum, it's routine to include the SOW so potential bidders can assess their interest in performing the work. If Section L, Instructions to Bidders, and Section M, Evaluation Criteria are included, you are armed with sufficient information to begin developing your WIN theme, discussed in Chapter 7, and detailed proposal outline. A Draft RFP also helps you identify long-lead items that need to be dealt with in advance of Final RFP Release. If the solicitation falls into the category of "must-WIN," it's advisable to begin investing time on the proposal effort immediately. Large companies may invest up to 60% of their proposal resources in advance of receiving the final RFP. If the upcoming solicitation falls into the must-win or strategic direction categories, and you don't have the benefit of a Draft RFP, make every effort to obtain a copy of the existing contract. If this is a recurring contract, you may be able to obtain a copy of the RFP from the last competition. The previous and current RFP's are usually quite similar with changes frequently found in selected areas of new contract clauses and additional contract requirements.

STEP 6: Make Bid/No-Bid Decision

The importance of making the Bid/No-Bid decision is a critical concept. Small companies often ask me, "Joe, what one thing could we do to bolster our WIN-rate?" Without knowing very much about the company or their industry; if they are a small company, I unequivocally suggest they choose which opportunities to bid more judiciously and let the others pass by. Bidding on every RFP consumes precious *Bid & Proposal* (B&P) resources and exhausts your people who will be needed for upcoming must-WIN procurements. There are many methodologies for making the all-important Bid/No-Bid decision. I'll share two approaches here, but bear in mind, there are many others. For instance, in one of my live workshops, a participant commented that she never bids a job if her company does not have a relationship or presence with the client. I agree, lack of a client relationship could be a show-stopper influencing your decision on Core Support procurement where contract award will likely be made on best value and first-hand knowledge of the contractor Program Manager who will execute the contract. But, when pursuing City Support contracts, which are oftentimes awarded on low price, I feel the relationship component plays a smaller role. Figure 9 displays one set of Bid-No-Bid Decision Criteria.

Figure 9. EXAMPLE #1 Bid/No-Bid Decision Criteria

- Does the solicitation represent a strategic direction for your company?

- Do you possess the necessary skill mix AND past performance to develop a credible proposal?

- Do you have the time and resources to do a credible job of bidding this contract?

- Can you reshuffle your existing workload or afford outside help to make time to bid?

- Is it reasonable to believe you will be the only bidder, whereby, any proposal might win?

If your answer to any two or more of the above five questions is no, your decision should probably be a *No-Bid*. There are notable exceptions to this "rule of thumb." One is if procurement is in a strategic business development area you are penetrating for the first time and have not had sufficient time to execute a teaming agreement or hire the proper skill set to fill voids in your capabilities. You may choose to bid knowing your chances of winning are slim, but you anticipate gleaning sufficient information from your proposal debrief to warrant the investment of time and energy.

Figure 10 shows another example of a more detailed Bid/No-Bid evaluation. This kind of analysis is typically prepared by your Business Development Manager who attends small business conferences and networks with clients to obtain the necessary information to complete this form.

Figure 10. EXAMPLE #2 Bid/No-Bid Decision Criteria

Phase 1 Bid/No-Bid Decision Form
Sources of Information: SYNOPSIS Dated Jun 8
And Telcon with Contract Specialist: Cindy *TODAY*
Client: AFMC Directed Energy (DE) and Space Vehicles (SV) Directorate, Kirtland AFB, NM
Contract Title: Business & Staff Support (BASS) for existing contract.
Incumbent: TBD
New Contract: Business Resources & Support Services (BRASS)
Note: BRASS is the 2nd such support contract
SOC Requirements: Provide all administrative support and program management within DE and SV at Kirtland AFB

Contract IDIQ with Task Orders (TOs), *5 Year Contract, $49M, CPFF* or FFP TOs, *Best Value Award*

SOC Submission will determine if 8(a) set-aside based upon Capability Statement:

1. Proof of 8(a) Status
2. Expertise in areas of: Administrative Support, Financial Management, Program/Project Management, Program Control Support, Execution, Reporting
3. Also, Archival Support, Marketing, HR Liaison, Training, Acquisition Certification Manager, Protocol, Process Development & Documentation, Facility/Equipment Support, Technical Library Management, Mail Center Support and Public Affairs (PA) Support.
4. Demonstration of prior contract performance within last 3 years for #2 above.
5. Some positions require Security Clearances of at least SECRET.

SOC Submission Original & 2 Copies, Less than 15 pages, DUE in 15 calendar days, Jul 5

Contractor will not be reimbursed for response (Proposal Development) costs.

Strategy Issues:

1. What is the incumbent's *reputation*? Is there an *opportunity for a new contractor*?
2. Clearance requirements *above SECRET* could be a big problem. Need clarification of # of positions, types of positions, and clearance requirements.
3. What are the *incumbent's costs*? *Are we competitive*?
4. Incumbent's contract with example TOs – Easy, can probably get from CS
5. Cost Benchmark: Web search, through *FOIA*, LONG LEAD!
6. *We have relevant experience, but only providing lower labor categories*: Perhaps teaming or hiring a Company PM with more Relevant Experience at Program Management, Program Cost Control, Execution, and Reporting. *The need for Acquisition Certification,* or simply relevant job experience is unclear.
7. Reimbursable FFP TOs have *no fee*. What's the value of TO?
8. *Can we financially execute this contract?*
   Estimated Win Probability (EWP):
   EWP = Pro + Con Arguments to Bid + Estimated # of Potential Bidders + Competition Estimated S&Ws
   Estimated Profit from Fee =
   Estimated Costs to Bid =

Do the Estimated Profits Outweigh Costs to Bid? ......is this a factor in our decision?

Although there is a lot of information summarized on this form, there are a few entries which should attract you to this particular procurement. First of all, what attracted us to even consider this RFP? It's a recurring contract with an incumbent and this is the follow-on. It's an ID/IQ, Best Value award contract, which happens to be one of our strengths. As a professional service, recurring contract, a substantial investment in bidding now can reap rewards beyond the 5-year contract period of performance with this client and others. You may choose to not bid this contract, but could position yourself for the follow-on. Further, this kind of contract represents a trend within government to outsource business support functions and can open doors to similar opportunities elsewhere in government. In summary, this is an attractive opportunity with lots of long-term benefits.

Also, there are a several issues that could be show-stoppers causing you to not bid unless you can uncover solutions to some of the strategic issues. These issues will be discussed in greater detail in Chapter 6, STEP-8.

STEP 7: Form Draft Proposal Team

Although we're only working with the Draft RFP at this point, we would like to bid in a teaming arrangement with another company; our company would be the lead or prime contractor. If you are the subcontractor in this arrangement, the prime will dictate how business, agreements, etc. will be conducted. Figure 11 shows a standard organizational structure you can use to begin assembling the members of your team.

Figure 11. Proposal Team before RFP Release

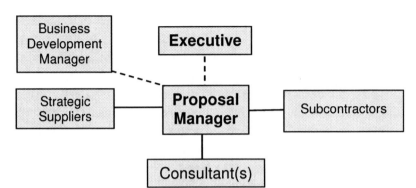

There may be six people involved in Business Development during Phase 1: the *Executive*, the *Business Development Manager* (BDM), the *Proposal Manager*, and, if needed, *Strategic Suppliers*, *Teaming Partners* (subcontractors) and *Consultants*. Most of these roles are strategic in nature (long-term) and while the Proposal Manager may not be involved until later, when it appears the company will bid the contract, we still need to orient the Proposal Manager to the upcoming solicitation in advance of receiving the RFP.

The Executive and Business Development Manager address the strategic issues of growth, company direction and what opportunities the company will pursue while overlooking others. The Proposal Manager may assist in developing the WIN Theme. Regardless, the BDM will provide the Proposal Manager with a Draft Executive Summary and WIN Theme while continuing to work strategic issues.

One example of a strategic issue the BDM may continue to work on includes identifying and preparing contracts for strategic suppliers and teaming partners. This is an interesting business environment we work in today. There once was a time when large companies would look down at small companies and competitors would offer a polite hello while passing you in the hall as if you two were boxers touching gloves before the big match. This has changed! Today it's not uncommon for government to set-aside a professional services contract for a small business with a much larger company providing hardware or technical support. In one case, a small business provides local installation and routine maintenance and support. They hold a strategic supplier agreement with Dell, Inc. computers for priority delivery to make government's ambitious contract delivery schedule. In this case, Dell knows they had no chance whatsoever of securing the prime contract role and is willing to be the subordinate. I see the same phenomena occurring where large companies like SAIC have coordinators whose sole purpose is to groom relationships with smaller companies so they can play a role as a subcontractor on set-aside contracts.

Consultants may be on your team for a variety of reasons. The most common include specialized technical expertise, short-term proposal assistance while your company staff is presently supporting a surge in workload, coaching for the delivery of oral proposals, or help positioning you for the next, must-WIN contract. More and more I see companies hiring consultants as an independent third party to determine existing client opinions and attitudes before it is documented as past performance. The advantage of using outside expertise is, they're paid for specific contributions and you benefit from that work long after the proposal is submitted; pay once and use many.

STEP 8: Develop WIN Strategy & Theme

This subject is so important and so often confused that I'll begin by offering my definition of WIN Strategy and WIN Theme. WIN Strategy includes the long-lead requirements that cannot be dealt with during the brief period of time when writing the proposal and hence must be addressed during Phase 1. Your WIN Theme includes the salient benefits of your proposal as compared to others that will give you a competitive edge. Chapter 7 will describe how to develop your WIN Theme.

The strategic issues that need to be addressed are listed below. They are an excerpt of the Bid/No-Bid worksheet prepared by the BDM in Figure 10 above.

Strategy Issues for BRASS Procurement:

1. What is the incumbent's *reputation*? Is there an *opportunity for a new contractor*?
2. Clearance requirements *above SECRET* could be a big problem. Need clarification of # of positions, types of positions, and clearance requirements.
3. What are the *incumbent's costs? Are we competitive*?
4. Incumbent's contract with example TOs – Easy, can probably get from CS
5. Cost Benchmark: Web search, through *FOIA*, LONG LEAD!
6. *We have relevant experience, but only providing lower level personnel*: Perhaps teaming or hiring a Company PM with more Relevant Experience at Program Management, Program Cost Control, Execution, and Reporting. *Need for Acquisition Certification,* or simply relevant job experience unclear.
7. Reimbursable FFP TO has *no fee*. What's the value of this TO?
8. *Can we financially execute this contract*?

Let's review these issues more closely to help us appreciate why they can influence our decision to bid or not-bid this contract.

In STEP 6 above, I described the advantages of this contract and how it holds long-term benefits for our company. On the flip side, there are some strategic, long-lead, issues which must be addressed immediately if you are to bid and WIN. First and foremost is understanding the reputation of the incumbent to ascertain if you can develop a theme to overtake them in the technical and management sections of the proposal. The fact that you must ask who the incumbent is tells me you may have overlooked this opportunity in your long-term planning. Also, our limited experience with security clearances above SECRET could impose too great a risk for the government. In trying to take this contract from the incumbent, you should know that whatever your proposal includes, you need to convince the client there will be a *seamless transition* to your management. There is no time to FOIA the Contracting Office so you will need to rely on your relationship with the CS to help you get a copy of the existing contract documentation, but it seems you may be too late. Unfortunately, with release of the Draft RFP, government is now in *blackout*. In blackout, all communication with the Contracting Office is formally submitted through the CO. Furthermore, any responses by the government are shared with all perspective bidders along with its question. Another shortfall that fits into the strategy area is the skill levels listed as requirements. You possess the management and technical talents to support the lower level jobs, but not the higher level skill sets; R&D Case Management, Program Management, etc.

In conclusion, shortfalls in the higher level skills, security clearances above SECRET and your inability to finance this level of effort contract imply you need to team with another company where we could compliment their strengths, most likely in a subcontractor role. Although this conclusion is disappointing, you will have similar opportunities in the future. If you had understood the incumbent and had the requisite time to address your shortfalls, you might have bid.

STEP 9: Draft Executive Summary

At this point you're seriously considering bidding the contract. The executive summary accomplishes the following:

- **Captures the essence of what makes you unique and creates focus**

- **Forms a baseline for your proposal**

- **Causes the evaluators to conclude, "Gee, they really understand us."**

- **Leads proposal evaluators to say, "If your proposal backs up what is described in your Executive Summary, you will WIN."**

The Draft Executive Summary in Figure 12 is written by the Business Development Manager and turned over to the Proposal Manager before the RFP arrives. It is a short summary of the main points of your offer aimed at the senior level decision-makers in the customer's organization. This important document, which may number only one to five pages, creates the focus for everyone who will contribute to the proposal. People are often reluctant to draft this document preferring to get started on the proposal and later see what comes of it. This approach, through frequently used, wastes time for very busy people writing pages and creating visuals that may not support the proposal that needs to be delivered just a few short weeks later. Because it is often so difficult to put pen to paper to create this important document, I've provided this fill-in-the-blank template in Figure 12 to use as a starting point.

Figure 12. Outline to Create a Draft Executive
          Summary

Summary Paragraph – *MyCompany* is the recognized leader
in ___. Our company employs___ with a solid reputation for
___. Some of our clients include ___. *MyCompany* is ___
owned Small Business headquartered in ___ and has been a
contractor to the federal government since ___. As such, we
enjoy a proven reputation for ___ and ___ within our
demanding industry.

Body of Executive Summary - emphasizes the key points of
your theme as it ties to the RFP Evaluation Criteria
e.g. Factor 2: Mission Capability, Subfactor 2: Management
Appropriate Theme Main Headings may include: (1) The
MyCompany Management Team; (2) Our Quality Culture; (3)
We Deliver Best Value; (4) We offer the low-risk solution.

Always close with – *MyCompany* is compliant with all of the
requirements in your solicitation. We offer the Low Risk, Best
Value solution to ___. We take no exceptions to the Terms
and Conditions of your solicitation.

STEP 10: Conduct Team Training

In advance of receiving the RFP I recommend two basic types of
training:

- Software

- Proposal

It's common for a small company to use Microsoft Word and
PowerPoint when desktop publishing their proposals. For
companies about to bid their first multi-year contract with $10
million in work per year, they may transition to more sophisticated
desktop publishing software better suited to a more professional
finished product.   Some popular packages include Microsoft

PageMaker and In Design. If you're making this change, have your people trained in advance of receiving the RFP. For those who will integrate information from numerous sources into the final format, I recommend conducting software training in advance of them actually being asked to apply these new skills. Also, another great time saver is having standard company templates for a single column, double column format and a standard format for visuals as well.

I strongly recommend proposal training for newcomers to your process. This can be done before the RFP is received although some companies successfully do this just-in-time, or when the skills are needed. I prefer newcomers be advised that they will be trained just before being asked to contribute. This alleviates a lot of uncertainty and its accompanying anxiety. The training conveys your company has an established process and lets them know where they will fit in, and most importantly, when they will be done. Everyone is already busy working other projects. Having this information helps belay some of the concerns they no doubt heard about being involved in a proposal effort. Employee training in one major ingredient that distinguishes the higher level companies from the Level 1 and 2 companies we cited in the Proposal Readiness Assessment in Section 3.3.

STEP 11: Update Library Resources

The ultimate goal of this section is to position you so that most of your time is spent refining an already good product. There are two main objectives. One is to consolidate and organize information into a ready access system for quick retrieval. The second is to have sufficient resources so that much of your proposal development becomes cut and splice with some rewriting to tailor your response to the specific RFP. It's far easier to rewrite than it is to create. Library resources may be housed in a physical file cabinet with folders. Today, this information is most often maintained on a secure server or laptop and includes the following information:

- ## Copies of past RFP's, proposals and proposal debriefs

- ## Consolidated resource of materials to allow users to quickly draw upon materials

- ## Research materials that may be used if you are surprised by an unexpected requirement in an RFP such as a Safety Plan, your company Quality Approach, your approach to project management, etc.

Some of the must haves include the following. This list includes sections you no doubt will be asked to provide in any proposal.

Organizational Chart and overview of your company - This is tailored to the new contract and may include an explanation of how your company was formed, the number of employees, your specialty, the areas in which you are highly regarded in the marketplace, your fast turn around, the tailored solutions which have saved clients both time and money, etc.

How you do business – To me this means a series of flow charts with accompanying narrative that describes how you deliver your product or service. Regardless of whether you're delivering a routinely manufactured item or delivering client-specific systems engineering solutions, you should have a process that describes the logical process from receipt of requirement, through delivery of the finished item or service. Another process flow chart describes how you ensure the integrity of your service delivery or the ultimate quality of your finished item. Each company has about a handful to a dozen key processes which allow them to function.

Management Content – This is a succinct description of how you hire, reward and develop your people. In today's environment where government looks for your Quality of Life formula for employee retention, this area is taking on more importance. There should also be a process for critiquing your work to ensure it reflects best-practices enjoyed throughout your industry. Many Architectural and Engineering firms sign-up for my training programs. This industry in particular has a professional association with a link on their home page to best practices. These companies learn from one another and quote the proven methods in their proposals.

Key Personnel – Most often Key Personnel may comprise the top 10% to 2-& of the personnel you're committing to the new contract. The credentials on their resumes should be eye watering and persuade the reader this team can start work tomorrow and do a great job. They're ready to go! Although government may only ask for resumes of Key Personnel, the more resumes you provide strengthens your position as being ready to do the work and reduces contract risk to the government. Although you typically have 30 days to phase in a new contract, any time spent orienting and refocusing the team rather than hiring gives you an edge shortly after contract award. If a key person retires or transfers, government wants to be notified of this impending vacancy and may even insist on playing some role in interviewing his or her replacement. Government wants to confirm the replacement is at least as well qualified as their predecessor.

Quality Assurance (QA) Approach – Whether delivering hardware, software or a service, some form of Quality Plan is required in almost any contract. The necessity of this feature of how your company does business is further amplified with the addition of Performance-Based Service Contracts in today's environment. In this case data are compiled and tracked against the government's Goals and Threshold figures for inclusion in monthly reports, quarterly program reviews with the client, etc.

How you Identify and Resolve Problems – This may be included in your Quality approach or the description of how you deliver your product or service. Here you describe how to perform reviews, analysis or testing to ensure problems are caught when they are small and can easily be corrected. In the A&E example I touched on earlier, firms go through a formal process of Preliminary and Final Design Reviews to catch small problems and refine the project design early on when the costs for changes are small. Even after signoff of the final design by government, there's yet another process for processing change orders to ensure the change doesn't conflict with other features of the overall design.

Resumes – This archive ensures you can easily select the necessary results to support the next contract by translating it into the format you will use in the proposal. Two points need to be made here. First, if you have a standard template for resumes and summarizing personnel information, it is likely many of the resumes could be tailored with little additional effort. For new resumes, it's far easier to edit down from a longer resume to fit your standard format than to make up information to fill the voids.

References for Past Performance – The information asked for by government varies in format, but is essentially the same from RFP to RFP. Whether you're asked to provide 3 or 5 references for past performance, be sure to choose references which are most closely related to this contract in terms of relevancy and scope. Furthermore, if the government PM or COR has moved onto another job, it's advisable to track down their new contact information lest your recommendation falls onto the desk of their replacement. The replacement probably does not have sufficient documentation or any motivation to give you a stellar rating. The tone of someone who has actually witnessed your style of work and ability to get the job done carries much more weight.

What does it Cost You to Do Business – If you have a baseline cost of doing business which you can adjust up or down to match the requirements of your new proposal you can easily generate an expected bid amount. Bottoms up estimates are far more time consuming and will rely on the technical and management people on the proposal to rush to turn material and manpower estimates into the cost estimator. This of course will need to be done later, but it can be comforting to know if your bid is even in a range of acceptability.

If you are used to bidding fixed price contracts where your cost accounting system does not have to be audited by an agency of the federal government, the transition to an approved system to support an upcoming negotiated contract is surely a long-lead item. It requires a considerable amount of time to prepare so you have succinct documentation describing your financial management approach that can be inserted into your proposal. Issues such as determining company Overhead, General & Administrative (G&A) Costs and an Indirect Labor Rate are difficult to address in a two to four week proposal without substantial preparation. Some solicitations grant you a period after award to bring your "Certified" accounting system online.

STEP 12: Plan for Proposal Facilities

The location dedicated to creating a proposal is frequently referred to as the *War Room*.

Proposal Writing – "a battle of competency with probably one victor where stamina and discipline will WIN!"

AUTHOR UNKNOWN

The proposal team does their work and statuses progress in the War Room. Anyone walking by the doorway of the War Room should know the people inside are working on something important that has great implications for the future of the company. Here are some recommendations:

- Facilities – quiet, comfortable room, which is detached from the daily routine so those involved in the proposal development are not distracted

- Meals and refreshments – convenient or in the room to make the best use of the teams valuable time (Buy lunch.)

- Computers and printers – detached from the larger, company LAN for security purposes and to ensure critical proposal sensitive information is not easily shared outside the War Room, (Be advised that corporate espionage is alive and well and you're advised to avoid using wireless communications on proposal projects.)

- Other equipment – should include fax, telephone and Internet connectivity through a dedicated computer for research purposes

- Work time – it should be stated clearly that everyone is expected to be present (8-5, 6 days a week to start, although I cannot recall one single proposal where I enjoyed the privilege of working an 8-hour day. On occasion I have stood beside the printer at midnight waiting for "that next draft" as we converged on the submission date. It's common for proposal team members to complete a full day working on the proposal and then return to their offices that evening to follow-up on urgent matters that simply cannot wait.)

In summary, Phase 1 is an important opportunity to gather the necessary information to help you decide to bid. Moreover, if you do choose to bid, you'll have sufficient information to tailor your proposal to the client. When reading your proposal, you want evaluators to say, "They really understand us."

Chapter 7.0 WIN Strategy and WIN Theme Development

Most Must-WIN contracts are already lost by the time the RFP comes out. That's because the right information was not collected and the right relationships were not developed in advance. The topics of strategy and theme in Phase 1 forces you to address the WIN and lose issues up front, before too many resources are expended on a contract you have little chance of WINning. If this process uncovers only one or two issues that can be dealt with before RFP release, you have time on your side to fill in the voids and develop a complete solution.

7.1 WIN Strategy

I will describe a successful strategy to WIN an upcoming procurement action in two categories; the overall WIN Strategy and the long-lead issues that must to be dealt with in advance of deciding to bid. Your strategy should match your capabilities and the contract requirements. Your strategy determines how you will use information in your theme throughout your proposal to persuade the proposal evaluator you are the one best suited for the job.

7.1.1 Overall WIN Strategy

Your strategy to secure a contract cannot simply state, "The incumbent can't deliver, but we can." But, you can delicately send a similar message knowing what proposal features are aligned with the clients thinking, and the concerns they have. This information was gathered earlier in Phase 1 through networking and organization/program research. The points in your theme alert the client to past problems, even disasters, that would be avoided by your approach. Seasoning your proposal with these remarks will enhance your reputation as someone fully understanding the inner workings of their organization and are able to remedy these past shortfalls. Furthermore, you're subliminally sending the message, "This bidder can do it all with flawless contract execution."

Your proposal is a sales document designed to convince the reader you are best suited to do the work. There are typically six different strategies you might employ to WIN. They are:

- Technical Approach
- Management Approach
- Competitive Approach
- Presentation Approach
- Cost Approach.
- Partnerships

Technical Approach – When claiming to deliver a superior technical solution, companies laud the superior capabilities of their people, unique test or manufacturing capability, one-of-a-kind research capability, time-tested process for translating broad client requirements into successful solutions, ISO Certification, or past performance on similar contracts.

Management Approach – Superior management may be conveyed by proposing a Program Manager with name and face recognition, a proven performer who is widely accepted as someone who not only gets the job done with finesse and grace, but allows everyone, both government and contractor alike, to feel they were part of a successful project. You may also tout your flat organization and ability to quickly identify issues and solve them while they are still inconsequential.

Competitive Approach – You can deliver the product or service, as well as any number of other companies can, but you do it in a superior manner. This is the result of your highly trained and specialized personnel and high employee retention rate, which presents the client with a consistent and capable team of familiar names and faces.

Presentation Approach – With oral proposals becoming more commonplace, this strategy is becoming increasingly important. Often it's a secondary strategy to WIN over the client. Here, companies rely on someone who is especially knowledgeable and skilled presenting before high-pressure groups and has a knack for handling the most difficult questions from the front of the room. Your insights will indicate if the group you'll present to prefers the polished marketer or the individuals who will actually perform the work. This seemingly small point addresses the preferences of the audience who at times prefer to hear directly from the people doing the work. This will begin to soften the barriers before moving onto the Question and Answer (Q&A) part of the presentation.

Cost Approach – If your SWOT Analysis showed you to be a premiere Best-Value service provider and you're preparing to bid a Firm Fixed-Price (FFP) Contract, you need to return to your SWOT results and extract your company's attributes that will support this kind of bid. This rewrite will present you as the low-cost, but high-quality, responsive service provider.

Partnerships – Teaming is a popular strategy today, is widely encouraged by government and labs alike. It's especially valuable when bidding to agencies that are aggressively bundling contracts. It allows you to not only offer the client a "turnkey" solution, but include proven specialists for each major requirement.

7.1.2 Example Strategy

Jaynes Corporation, a construction company, chose to present a superior technical solution; enhanced employee safety and low-cost. Jaynes knew competition would be great for the construction of a new Federal Aviation Administration (FAA) air traffic control tower. While other companies bid a traditional scaffolding system that would increase in height and complexity as the tower grew taller, Jaynes instead capitalized on the symmetry of the structures exterior surfaces. They designed a platform that would allow trades people unfettered access to the structure while each level was being constructed. The platform would then be raised to the next level. This method increased employee productivity, and shortened the project schedule, while reducing workers compensation charges, all contributing to a superior, lower-cost solution to the government.

I'm frequently asked by small companies, "What's the best way to compete for government contracts?" The answer is easy, "You want to *avoid* or *limit* competition if at all possible." I can think of a woman-owned company in Los Angeles who sought my advice when reviewing a Request for Information (RFI) for professional counselors to help military families at Camp Pendleton, CA, whose spouses were deployed overseas. In this instance, the Navy was trying to bundle several such contracts to support multiple military installations. Thanks to this quick-acting entrepreneur, she was able to persuade the CO, with the help of her local SBA, to make the Camp Pendleton portion of the service a set-aside contract for woman-owned businesses. So if you're unable to influence a contract change to a sole-source contract, you can at lease limit the competition to a set-aside category where you're competing head-to-head with similar-sized companies.

A strategy question frequent asked is, "We're new to the government contracts market, what's a good way to start?" This answer depends on the type of product or service the company has to offer, but generally it's best to start with a GSA Schedule Contract or subcontract through a Prime Contractor on a fixed-price contract. I recommend these two options because the smallest company, given the time, can review the GSA web site and figure out how to bid on their own without outside assistance making both their investment and risk low. Subbing to another company on a fixed price contract helps you become familiar with the manner of doing business with government; you learn the vocabulary and the nuances of interacting with government. Because it's fixed-price, you're not encumbered by needing the certified accounting system required on larger, cost-reimbursement-type contracts. Over time, this experience will help you choose which types of contracts you're best suited to bid in the future. Also, because you're a sub, your risk of being affected by an adverse *Contractor Performance Assessment Reporting System* (CPARS) report is minimal. As a sub, you may cite contracts you contributed to, but explain which parts of the contract scope you actually did perform. This can distance you and explain why your part of the work was not downgraded in the government's report while the prime and overall contract were. The role and importance of Past Performance will be described in Chapter 11.

7.2 Long-Lead Strategy Issues

Strategy issues that may require long-lead times include gathering information through a FOIA request. By long-lead I'm referring to research, coordination, or work that simply cannot be accomplished during that brief 2, 4 or 6 week period you have to create your proposal. If you're bidding to DOE or a national laboratory that requires an Integrated Safety Management Plan

(ISMP), this too could be a long-lead item requiring extensive research in advance of receiving the RFP. Identifying potential competitors and teaming partners is a long-lead item if you have no past experience with how long it might take them to tailor and process a teaming agreement through their legal representative.

Some must-do's in almost any strategy should include overcoming shortfalls in past performance. So, if you received a less than stellar CPARS report, you should at a minimum submit a response through that contract CO to either rebut or explain a client's low rating. Mending fences of damaged relationships with PMs, COs and CSs is also a long-lead item. The bottom line is that every company has their foibles. It's not fatal to have slipped up in the past; however, it can be very hazardous to your Past Performance evaluation if you repeat the same problems contract after contract and you appear to be unable to remedy the problem. But remember, the proposal you're now writing is a description of *how you will* conduct business on this new contract, not how you've done business in the past.

Acknowledge your shortfalls and deliver a plausible explanation in this new proposal to demonstrate you're capable of doing better. One example is turning monthly reports in on time. This is a small point; but on-time delivery is something that's easy for the government to measure. Your new proposal may have a paragraph titled, "Our Timely Reporting System." In it you describe your system for generating reports, their lead time and assigned responsibility to surface in routine in-house Staff Meetings. There should be a specific milestone, assignment of responsibility and visibility to management within your company. Government is searching for your system, your management approach, your tickler file; those things in your company that would suggest flawless execution of the contract. If you can do the little things well, there is an inference you can do everything else well too.

7.2.1 BRASS Strategy Issues

In Figure 10 we described a second example of how to conduct a Bid/No-Bid Decision. In that example, the BDM cited several strategy issues that, if not addressed, could clearly make this procurement decision a No-Bid. Given the benefit of time, either through a Draft RFP, the preceding contract documentation through FOIA, or some other means, you can buy valuable time to remedy these shortcomings. Be advised, the earlier you ask questions of government contracting and program personnel before Blackout, the more likely that you will be able to secure this information.

The long-lead, or strategy, items identified for BRASS in Figure 10 include:

- What is the incumbent's reputation? Is there an opportunity for a new contractor?

- Clearance requirements *above SECRET* could be a serious problem. We need clarification of the number of positions, types of positions, and clearance requirements.

- What are the incumbent's costs? Are we competitive?

- Incumbent's contract with example TOs – Easy to get, can probably obtain from CS.

- Cost Benchmark: Web search, through *FOIA*, LONG LEAD TIME!

- *Have relevant experience, but with supporting lower level personnel*: Teaming, maybe new PM with more relevant experience at program management, program cost control, execution, and reporting may be required. Do the people maintaining the government's system of

Acquisition Certification require us to be certified as well or is relevant job experience adequate?

- Reimbursable FFP TO has *no fee*. What's the value of this TO?

- Can we financially execute this contract?

You should surmise from this list of eight issues that you are simply not prepared to bid at this time. But, a rigorous process of information gathering may lead you to a credible proposal submission. Gathering this information on a compressed schedule will be time consuming and, hence, expensive. So it is important to note that not asking the right questions early in Phase 1 will make bidding more costly and also jeopardize your chances of WINning.

7.3 WIN Theme

Developing your Theme is an exercise in organization, consistency and follow-through. Like the SWOT Analysis, it is a facilitated exercise, but focuses on the contract you're preparing to bid. Theme points are displayed in several locations throughout your proposal, therefore it merits great attention. Some proposal evaluators say, "If your proposal substantiates the claims you made in your Executive Summary, you will probably WIN." So your Executive Summary, and brief summaries at the beginning of each section of your proposal, stating the main points of your strategy and are reinforced with additional, substantiating points so the reader can discover the logical conclusion that you are the obvious, inevitable WINner. You're helping the reader "connect the dots."

Table 12 displays the results of a brief exercise to develop the specific points you will include in your proposal to answer the question, "Why should government award us this contract?" As you can see, your strengths, weaknesses, and competitor information (threats) may be derived from your last SWOT exercise making this a good place to start, and then tailor it for this particular contract. It's important to address your competitor's strengths and weaknesses at this time. Companies preparing to bid a contract typically spend lots of time focusing on how they could WIN; so much time, in fact, they frequently overlook how they might lose.

Three specific questions that arise from Table 11:

- **How do you expand on your strategy claim to offer your client the low-risk solution?**

- **How do you overcome a known weakness?**

- **How do you capitalize on competitor shortcomings?**

How do you expand on your strategy claim to offer your client the low-risk solution? – The statement you offer the client will include the low-risk solution in the summary remarks at the beginning of selected proposal sections and of course the executive summary. You now need to substantiate your claim. This is from your strengths listed in Table 10, explaining to the reader why these points contribute to your claim of being the low-risk approach.

Table 11.   WIN Theme Development

Understanding *MyCompany*

My Strengths	*My* Weaknesses	How to Overcome *My* Weaknesses
Consistent high-quality delivery performance Rapid response capability Multiple industry experience Very client oriented	Limited higher level skills *Smaller Business*	Possible joint effort or teaming *Use as a strength Agile & responsive*

Understanding *My* Competition

Their Strengths	*Their* Weaknesses	How to Exploit *Their* Weaknesses
Larger business, with more people resources *As incumbent possess "inside track"*	*"Trust us" approach* *"Can't manage large projects to save their life"*	*Capitalize on our strength in this area*

This may be handled in the following manner:

- Our consistent, high-quality delivery performance, as demonstrated in our Past Performance, clearly indicates *MyCompany* can deliver as promised – This remark may be included in the management, quality, or past performance sections of your proposal.

- *MyCompany's* vast experience in this and related industries, shows we can anticipate and account for surprises and changes in requirements, while meeting demanding, client-imposed delivery milestones – This may be included in a discussion of your process to conduct technical work, in the management section or past performance section.

- Our rapid response capability has been field tested, demonstrates the highly-trained, responsive and well-resourced teams we deploy on short notice – This may be included in human resource, management, or business process section.

- Our flat organizational structure and client-focused business model ensures small challenges will be identified early in the program. Through open, frequent lines of communication and client participation, we can quickly move from project concept to final review with an informed client approval – This may be included in management or technical process section.

How do you overcome a known weakness? – I cited two company weaknesses in Table 12; you possess limited higher level skilled personnel and your business is much smaller than the incumbent. First, your limited skill mix may be overcome by teaming with another company. The second point, your small size, can be handled differently. I suggest your size is not a weakness, rather it is a strength. Because of your size, you are agile and responsive to last-minute changes, and possess responsive systems to handle these eventualities. Furthermore, when you are awarded this contract, it will represent one of the largest contracts in your business base. Therefore, the client will enjoy the full support of top management on those infrequent occasions when the company Program Manager seeks additional resources to support surges in workload. Point out to the reader that what might be a small and unimportant project to larger companies is very important to you. Be advised, your size must be dealt with delicately in your proposal or it could be interpreted as imparting additional contract risk to the client. Please note both of these possible solutions are long-lead.

How do you capitalize on competitor shortcomings? – It would be so easy to say, "We can do the work and they can't," but it simply isn't done that way. You cannot create the appearance that you're making a direct attack on another company, but you must tactfully address their shortcomings if they are your strengths. In this case you *ghost* the competition.

In Table 12, under Competitor Weaknesses you uncovered, through intelligence gathering, that the client feels the incumbent does a good job managing smaller projects, but has difficulty managing larger ones. You can appreciate this shortcoming if the need for a highly skilled Project Manager is repeated throughout the solicitation and the shortfall with the incumbent was corroborated by others within government. In this instance you undoubtedly will have a section in your proposal titled, "Our Proven Approach to Project Management." This section can include the following points:

- Describe the process for selecting future Project Managers.

- Describe your mentoring approach to groom entry-level PMs for increasing levels of responsibility.

- Describe your rewards and recognition system to acknowledge excellence in Project Management and keeping the client informed and happy.

- Describe your rigorous educational requirements for developing PMs relying on industry-recognized certification standards such as the Project Management Institute.

7.3.1 Example Theme

In the Jaynes Corporation example, 7.1.2, the detailed Theme points may be as shown below. Note that I have also identified which part of your proposal this information should apply to; e.g., leadership, safety, management, technical processes, cost, teamwork, etc.

- Jaynes "People First Policy" for employee safety is the driving force behind all of our construction solutions. – Leadership and Safety

- We'll deliver on an accelerated project schedule with no additional project risk. – Management

- We have lower project cost through innovative and safer solutions. – Management, Technical Process, and Cost

- The same teamwork and innovation that resulted in our platform solution will be applied in the field as new challenges arise. – Teamwork and Management

- We maintain a cadre of highly trained Project Managers who are certified through the Project Management Institute's rigorous requirements. – Management and Human Resource Development

- Jaynes mentoring approach to develop Project Managers with increasing levels of responsibility has been developed through more than 20 years of construction management excellence. – Management and Human Resource Development

Here are a few choice words that may help get you get started developing your next WIN Theme:

• Employee-owned	• Reliable
• Innovative	• Seamless
• Efficiency	• Scalable
• Not distracted by acquisitions and mergers	• Meets or exceeds performance standards
• Responsive	• Award-winning
• Lower cost	• Financially sound
• ISO 9000 certified	

In closing, everything I presented in this chapter can be done by you in your company. It's simply a bookkeeping exercise in understanding the strengths and weaknesses of your company, having sufficient time to overcome noted weaknesses and having strategy and theme tightly interconnected to deliver a credible proposal that ties together well and makes for easy reading.

Chapter 8.0 Proposal Development
(Phase 2)

People typically associate proposal development with sitting down and writing the actual proposal. Although my Five-Phase Approach™ helps you step back and look at the broader point of view, this phase remains the centerpiece for earning government business. It's where all of the information you've gathered and distilled is applied. The proposal you submit to government creates the first impression of how your company is viewed by proposal evaluators. If your proposal is well organized, easy to follow, thorough, and professionally done, it will establish expectations for the quality of work you will perform after contract award.

To give this important subject the attention it deserves, I've divided the entire proposal development process into three straightforward chapters: 8, 9 and 10. Throughout this material I'll describe the process, typical sticking in points and suggestions to enhance your proposal.

By now, after reviewing Phase 1, Marketing to Government and Preparing to receive the RFP, you should have a better understanding of the activities that occur in advance of your receiving the RFP that will make you successful here in Phase 2. Before we begin, let's take a brief glimpse of what a failing Proposal Team "looks like."

8.1 Symptoms of a Failing Proposal Team

The purpose of this section is to review what a proposal effort looks like when we lack the requisite leadership, organization, training, and discipline. I'm speaking of the Level-1 companies briefly introduced in Section 3.3. The symptoms of a Level-1 company proposal effort look something like this.

- Team suffers through frustration, lack of sleep, endless disagreements, and humiliating proposal reviews, if there are any reviews at all.

- No Bid & Proposal (B&P) monies have been set aside for this effort, therefore simple chargeable tasks, such as reproductions, become an accounting juggling act.

- Without a clear plan of action, team members prematurely start writing paragraphs and sections that simply do not convey a coherent message.

- Proposal page count is two or three times the allowable limit.

- Graphics are not consistently formatted and are unintelligible.

- If they had a proposal schedule, they would see that there's no time left for an end-to-end review of their work. Instead, the schedule is replaced with gut-wrenching anxiety.

- Staff cannot sleep through the night because they get up numerous times to jot down ideas.

- Cold pizza.

In proposal development, as in War, there is often a thin, fragile line separating control from utter chaos, and tides can turn in the blink of an eye. What's needed is a consistent, uniform process that creates a final product you are proud of and will WIN. Having a well-defined process helps the team members "see" what needs to be done, by when, and how all of the pieces will come together. Most importantly, having a process reduces stress for all involved by conveying when we will be done with a clear path to get there. The client is trying to award the contract to the offeror who earned the last 50 or 100 points out of a 1,000. That should tell us it's the refined, polished proposal that WINs. Moreover, a team operating in a reactive mode creates more work, not less.

8.2 17-Step Proposal Development Process Overview

The 17-step process for proposal development is displayed in Figure 13. The process has a well-defined beginning, middle, and end. It begins with receipt of the RFP and ends with your WINning proposal being received by the client. In between, there is a well-choreographed series of events managed by the Proposal Manager to deliver the message that you are uniquely qualified to perform this work. Here, marketing and intelligence information from Phase 1 is condensed, processed, and assembled to present a coherent message. The objective of this detailed step-by-step process is to ensure all RFP requirements are met, decision-points are obvious, reduced stress for you and your proposal teammates, everyone knows how they fit into the process and how each will contribute. Most importantly, everyone will know when they have completed their part so they can confidently return to other, billable work. Subsequent sections of Chapters 8, 9, and 10 will describe each of the 17-Steps in detail. Be advised, this methodology will not allow you to go home early. It will help avoid major last minute rewrites and refocus wasted time toward refining an already good product. It will also help you sleep at night.

148

Figure 13. 17-Step Proposal Development Process

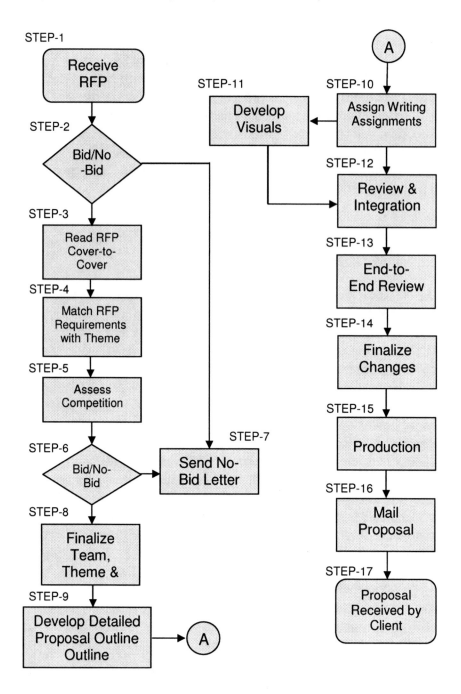

STEP 1: Receive RFP

Immediately upon receiving the RFP, distribute copies of the entire solicitation to the core team from Phase 1. This includes the Executive, Business Development Manager (BDM), Proposal Manager, Strategic Suppliers, Subcontractors, and Consultants, if any. Also, provide copies to an SME in contracts and accounting. The team is growing and will soon be able to provide the necessary information for an informed decision to bid. Each team member quickly reviews the solicitation.

A kick-off meeting then follows to work through STEPS 2 - 8 below; Quick Bid/No-Bid Decision through Finalize Proposal Team, Theme and Schedule, after everyone has had an opportunity to review the solicitation. Here, the Proposal Manager builds the contact list to include team member names, home and office phone, cell, email addresses, and a comment on the best way to reach them. Although there are several steps to address, this part of the process goes quickly. If you had the benefit if a DRAFT RFP, look closely at what has changed. If you did not have the benefit of a DRAFT, move onto STEP 2.

STEP 2: Bid/No-Bid Decision

"Why does my boss keep making promises I can't keep?"

AUTHOR UNKNOWN

Every proposal represents a serious commitment. This not only includes the time and money you'll invest in bidding the contract, but also a pledge to do the work, inasmuch as the agency can sometimes turn your proposal into a contract with the simple addition of a government signature.

After the core team skims through the RFP, they proceed with STEP 2, the Bid/No-Bid Decision. If you had the benefit of a

Draft RFP you may scan the Final RFP for noteworthy changes that may influence your decision whether to bid or not. If the RFP looks similar enough to merit investing more time, we move onto STEP 3. If you did not have the benefit of a Draft RFP then ask the basic questions below to determine if there is any merit in moving further. Also, any major change in the RFP requires another Bid/No-Bid decision.

Figure 14. Bid/No-Bid Decision Making

Question 1: Is the SOW in this RFP consistent with what your company does?

Question 2: Is the SOW in the RFP consistent with a strategic direction in which your company is growing?

Question 3: If you look at the estimated value of the contract, your chances of WINning, the cost to bid the contract, and your anticipated profit or fee, do the numbers infer that you should bid?

Question 4: Do you have the fiscal and manpower resources to bid the job or are you too busy right now?

If your answer to each of questions 1 through 4 above is No, then there's no decision to be made. You simply send a No-Bid Letter to the CS. Otherwise, you have a decision to make. Typically a decision to bid is still made when your answer to Question 4 is No because the company business development person better understands the future workload for the company and can conclude, "we may be too busy to bid right now, but we're really going to need this work two years out." If your answer to Questions 1 and 2 are No then it's clear to me that you should not bid, but I have been out-voted in the past.

If you pass that first test, you may want to consider the estimated value of the contract. Be advised that the estimated contract value provided in the solicitation is merely a government estimate. In my personal experience, I've seen government estimates as much as five times too high. So the contract dollars actually applied to the contract could be only one-fifth of what was quoted in the government estimate. So beware! This is where the value of your relationship with the client, your professional community, and the intelligence gathered in Phase 1 influence your judgment. If other contracts from this client have been woefully under estimated in the past, there's a chance the new contract is underestimated as well. The best estimate is typically on recurring contracts. In this case, government merely reviews past invoices and makes adjustments for changes in requirements; These estimates are usually fairly reliable.

STEP 3: Read the RFP from Cover-to-Cover

Reading the RFP can be intimidating. With its own unique vocabulary and seeming duplication of information, it can be daunting for new people involved in business development. Even seasoned professionals can find themselves in unfamiliar territory when reading an RFP from an agency they have previously not done business with. Digesting and applying Sections A-M is a lot like the game rule book in sports. Your every move must comply with a specific set of rules under the watchful eye of a referee on the field. You too must comply with the game book (the solicitation sections) when developing your proposal. Sections A-M are your rule book, and it is the team who can work best within these rules that will WIN the day.

I recommend locking yourself in a quiet room to read the RFP from cover-to-cover. You're preparing to meet with the others on the proposal team to make important decisions related to your WIN theme, how your strengths match the solicitations requirements, and who else needs to be added to the team to round out the list of contributors, as well as the all-important decision to bid.

After reading the RFP you're armed with your questions. The cover sheet of your RFP, the SF33, tells you who will take your questions. Be prudent when asking questions because your competitors will be given copies of your questions along with the government's response. One example question is as follows:

> Instructions to the offeror in Section-L states, "the cost volume will be delivered on one-disk." It then goes onto say, "the second disc will include ___ and the third disc will include ___." Please clarify the number of discs and their contents for the Cost Proposal submission.

STEP 3 addresses one of the frequent complaints I hear from proposal evaluators in government and the national labs. They complain, "It's evident from reading proposals that the offeror did not read or possibly did not understand the requirements." Your proposal is intended to impress and persuade the government to award you a contract. Please don't overlook the basics by making your client read three-fourths of your proposal before concluding you cannot support all of the mandatory requirements, and hence, are not qualified to bid. So this is an important step. When reading the solicitation look for the following:

- Requirements that can easily be addressed by drawing from your Resource Library with some tailoring.

- Requirements that you are simply not prepared to address, therefore requiring substantial research to respond to or teaming with a new partner or consultant with the requisite specialized knowledge to fill the void. In either case, this is a long-lead item that requires your immediate attention if you decide to bid.

- Are there any contract clauses you take exception to? Someone from your contracts office could quickly put your concerns to rest or affirm that a particular contract clause will be difficult for your company to accommodate. This is an important topic, as the clauses will become part of your contract.

- Are there any parts of the RFP that need clarification that may require you to submit a formal question though the CO or CS? Instructions on how to submit clarifying questions are included in Section L of the RFP. One example of such a statement in the solicitation is shown below to assist you in turning in the proper information with your proposal.

Below is a sample listing of the Sections I extracted from the BRASS RFP for instructional purposes. You can obtain a complete copy of the entire BRASS solicitation by visiting my web site at: www.proposalw.com and clicking on FREE Downloads.

Let's review the salient features of what you should glean from reading the RFP from cover-to-cover. Note that the INTERPRETATION paragraph after each BRASS section is intended to convey the essence of what government is trying to convey. I also underlined the portions of the section I'm referring to.

8.3.1 SECTION A-SOLICITATION, OFFER AND AWARD, SF33

The Standard Form 33 (SF33) in Figure 15 is a single-page form designed to be the cover sheet of a solicitation. After your company's designated representative signs it, your attached proposal becomes an offer. After all offers are reviewed, the government may then go into negotiations or choose to simply sign below your name on the SF33 making the attached contract documentation a binding contract.

Some noteworthy BLOCKS on this form are as follows:

- BLOCK 4: identifies this will be a negotiated contract as opposed to a sealed bid-type contract.

- BLOCK 10: identifies Cynthia as the Contract Specialist whom you may contact for this solicitation.

- BLOCK 11: includes the table of contents where you inventory all of the sections and pages you've downloaded to ensure you have the entire document.

- BLOCK 12: here government asks that your proposal, including price/cost, remain good for 120 calendar days. This suggests it may take government that much time to review proposals and make a contract award. Cost your proposal accordingly to account for this time.

- BLOCK 13: identifies the percentage discount you are willing to offer the government for prompt payment of your invoices.

- BLOCK 14: you acknowledge you received all of the solicitation amendments so all offerors are bidding to the latest requirements.

- BLOCK 15: is your company information and identification of the person who is authorized to sign on behalf of your company and authorize contractual commitments.

Figure 15: Solicitation, Offer and Award, Standard Form 33 (SF33) NOTE: On two pages

SOLICITATION, OFFER AND AWARD	1. THIS CONTRACT IS A RATED ORDER UNDER DPAS (15 CFR 350)	RATING DO-C9	PAGE OF PAGES 1
2. CONTRACT NO.	3. SOLICITATION NO. **FA9451-05-R-0003** CODE FA9451	4. TYPE OF SOLICITATION ☐ SEALED BID (IFB) ☒ NEGOTIATED (RFP)	5. DATE ISSUED	6. REQUISITION/PURCHASE NO.

7. ISSUED BY AFRL/PK8DB
AF RESEARCH LABORATORY (DET 8)
2251 MAXWELL AVE., SE
KIRTLAND AFB, NM 87117-5773
CYNTHIA XXXXXXX, 505-846-XXXX
CYNTHIA.XXXXXXXX@KIRTLAND.AF.MIL

8. ADDRESS OFFER TO (If other than Item 7)

NOTE: In sealed bid solicitations "offer" and "offeror" mean "bid" and "bidder".

SOLICITATION

9.

10. FOR INFORMATION CALL:	A. NAME See Block 7	B. TELEPHONE (Include area code) (NO COLLECT CALLS) See Block 7	C. E-MAIL ADDRESS See Block 7

11. TABLE OF CONTENTS

(√)	SEC.	DESCRIPTION	PAGE(S)	(√)	SEC	DESCRIPTION	PAGE(S)
		PART I - THE SCHEDULE				PART II - CONTRACT CLAUSES	
√	A	SOLICITATION/CONTRACT FORM	1	√	I	CONTRACT CLAUSES	15
√	B	SUPPLIES OR SERVICES AND PRICES/COSTS	2			PART III - LIST OF DOCUMENTS, EXHIBITS, AND OTHER ATTACH.	
√	C	DESCRIPTION/SPECS./WORK STATEMENT	5	√	J	LIST OF ATTACHMENTS	22
√	D	PACKAGING AND MARKING	6			PART IV - REPRESENTATIONS AND INSTRUCTIONS	
√	E	INSPECTION AND ACCEPTANCE	7	√	K	REPRESENTATIONS, CERTIFICATIONS,	K - 1
√	F	DELIVERIES OR PERFORMANCE	8			AND OTHER STATEMENTS OF OFFERORS	
√	G	CONTRACT ADMINISTRATION DATA	10	√	L	INSTRS, CONDS, AND NOTICES TO OFFERORS	L - 1

| √ | H | SPECIAL CONTRACT REQUIREMENTS | 12 | √ | M | EVALUATION FACTORS FOR AWARD | M - 1 |

OFFER (Must be fully completed by offeror)

NOTE: Item 12 does not apply if the solicitation includes the provisions at 52.214-16, Minimum Bid Acceptance Period.

12. In compliance with the above, the undersigned agrees, if this offer is accepted within **120** calendar days *(60 calendar days unless a different period is inserted by the offeror)* from the date of receipt of offers specified above, to furnish any or all items upon which prices are offered at the price set opposite each item, delivered at the designated point(s), within the time specified in the schedule.

13. DISCOUNT FOR PROMPT PAYMENT (See Section I, Clause No. 52.232-8) 🢁	10 CALENDAR DAYS %	20 CALENDAR DAYS %	30 CALENDAR DAYS %	CALENDAR DAYS %

14. ACKNOWLEDGEMENTS OF AMENDMENTS *(The offeror acknowledges receipt of amendments to the SOLICITATION for offerors and related documents numbered and dated:*	AMENDMENT NO.	DATE	AMENDMENT NO.	DATE

15A. NAME AND ADDRESS OF OFFEROR	CODE		FACILITY		16. NAME AND TITLE OF PERSON AUTHORIZED TO SIGN OFFER *(Type or print)*

15B. TELEPHONE NO. *(Include area code)*	15C. CHECK IF REMITTANCE ADDRESS IS DIFFERENT FROM ABOVE - ENTER SUCH ADDRESS IN SCHEDULE. ☐	17. SIGNATURE	18. OFFER DATE

AWARD (To be completed by Government)

19. ACCEPTED AS TO ITEMS NUMBERED	20. AMOUNT	21. ACCOUNTING AND APPROPRIATION

22. AUTHORITY FOR USING OTHER THAN FULL AND OPEN COMPETITION: ☒ 10 U.S.C. 2304(c) (5) ☐ 41 U.S.C. 253(c) ( )	23. SUBMIT INVOICES TO ADDRESS SHOWN IN 🢁 *(4 copies unless otherwise specified)*	ITEM

24. ADMINISTERED BY *(If other than Item 7)* CODE	25. PAYMENT WILL BE MADE BY	CODE

26. NAME OF CONTRACTING OFFICER *(Type or print)*	27. UNITED STATES OF AMERICA *(Signature of Contracting Officer)*	28. AWARD DATE

IMPORTANT - Award will be made on this Form, or on Standard Form 26, or by other authorized official written notice.

Standard Form 33

8.3.2 SECTION B - SUPPLIES OR SERVICES AND PRICES/COSTS

ITEM	SUPPLIES OR SERVICES	Qty Purch	Unit	Unit Price Total Item Amount
0001				_____

<table>
<tr><td>Noun:</td><td>BUSINESS RESOURCES and SUPPORT SERVICES</td></tr>
<tr><td>ACRN:</td><td>U</td></tr>
<tr><td>Contract type:</td><td>J - FIRM FIXED PRICE</td></tr>
<tr><td>Start Date:</td><td>AS REQUIRED</td></tr>
<tr><td>Completion Date:</td><td>AS REQUIRED</td></tr>
<tr><td>Descriptive Data:</td><td></td></tr>
</table>

The contractor shall furnish all personnel, services, supervision and all other items necessary to accomplish the tasks defined in the performance work statement (PWS) entitled "Business Resources and Support Services (BRASS)" hereby incorporated as attachment #1. Task orders will be issued in accordance with the Section H clause, entitled "Ordering Procedures". Basic period of performance is five years from the date of award.

INTERPETATION: There are 5 Contract Line Item Numbers (CLINs) that must be estimated to secure this contract. CLIN 0001, shown above, represents an estimate to perform the contract's baseline management and administration of the contract for a period of 5 years. The two price entries above for Unit Price and Total Item Amount will, in this case, be the same numerical figure including all costs, overhead, fee, and state Gross Receipts Tax to accomplish the work over the five-year period of performance. Manpower estimates were provided by government based upon historical figures.

8.3.3 SECTION B – SUPPLIES OR SERVICES AND PRICES/COSTS

8.3.3.1 B060 TRANSITION/PHASE-IN AND PHASE-OUT PERIODS

> If a non-incumbent is the successful offeror, the non-incumbent shall be required to use the government-designated Transition/Phase-In period of no more than 30 calendar days to familiarize itself with the contractual obligations and requirements in preparation for total assumption of responsibilities. Phase-In shall be in accordance with the requirements of the solicitation (reference performance work statement, Section J), and the non-incumbent's approved Phase-In Plan which must be submitted with its proposal. Accordingly, at the end of the contract, a Transition/Phase-Out Period of no more than 30 calendar days may also be required for the same purpose.

INTERPETATION: Some version of this clause is included in all recurring contracts. If a contractor, other than the incumbent, WINs the follow-on contract, they will typically be allowed 30 calendar days to phase in and be fully functioning under the new contract, this 30-day period must be reflected in the contractor's Phase-In plan and schedule. CLIN 0004 pays for new contractor Phase In. This is a good time to mention that the proposal evaluators will be specifically looking for your *seamless transition* to prevent any interruption in service during contract turnover.

8.3.4 SECTION C – DESCRIPTION /SPECS/WORK STATEMENT

> CONTRACT LINE ITEM NUMBERS (CLINs) 0001-0005 should be performed in accordance with Government performance work statement entitled "Business Resources and Support Services (BRASS)" hereby incorporated as attachment #1, reference section J of the contract.

INTERPETATION: There are five CLINs for this contract. This section refers you to Section J of the solicitation where Attachment #1 contains the Performance Work Statement (PWS), detailed requirements, for CLIN 0001 you will bid to.

8.3.5 SECTION D – PACKAGING AND MARKINGS

NO CLAUSES OR PROVISIONS IN THIS SECTION

INTERPETATION: The contractor deliverables under this contract includes studies, analysis, and administrative and management reports. As such, there are no special packaging requirements. Markings, which you would expect to be included in this Section, are included below in Section F, F005: Delivery of Reports.

8.3.6 E007 INSPECTION AND ACCEPTANCE AUTHORITY (TAILORED)

Inspection and acceptance for all Contract and Exhibit Lines or Subline Items shall be accomplished by the Contracting Officer's Representative (COR) , Mr. Eric XXXX (505) 846-XXXX, AFRL/DEL, 3550 Aberdeen Avenue SE Kirtland AFB NM 87117-5776.

INTERPRETATION: As is typically the case, it is the responsibility of the COR to accept contractor deliverables and make a judgment as to their acceptability. Then an information copy is sent to the Contracting Officer (CO) as described in F005 below.

8.3.7 SECTION F - DELIVERIES/PERFORMANCE

F005 DELIVERY OF REPORTS (TAILORED)

> (b) <u>All reports and correspondence</u> submitted under this contract <u>shall include the contract number and project number</u> and be forwarded <u>prepaid</u>. A copy of the letters of <u>transmittal shall be delivered to the Procuring Contracting Officer (PCO) and Administrative Contracting Officer (ACO)</u>. The addresses are set forth on the contract award cover page. All other address(es) and code(s) for consignee(s) are as set forth in the contract or incorporated by reference.

INTERPRETATION: This clause acknowledges the distribution list the contractor will follow to submit the proper number of report copies and to whom. The Procurement Contracting Officer (PCO) is a CO in the Contracting Office with signature authority to sign off on the contract award. The Administrative Contracting Officer (ACO) administers the contract after the award, including changes and modifications with signature authority. Often the PCO becomes the ACO after contract award.

8.3.8 SECTION G – CONTRACT ADMINISTRATION DATA

G018 CONTRACT HOLIDAYS (TAILORED)

> (a) The prices/costs in Section B of the contract include holiday observances; accordingly, the Government will not be billed for such holidays, except when services are required by the Government and are actually performed on a holiday. Holidays in addition to those reflected in this contract, which are designated by the Government, will be billable provided the assigned Contractor employee was available for performance and was precluded from such performance.

INTERPETATION: This clause is commonplace in professional services contracts. Essentially, the client desires your people to be on site when the government is working and follow their Holiday schedule. Some bidders choose to set up new companies for this kind of bid where time off and overhead rates could differ from the parent company's benefit and compensation package.

8.3.9 SECTION H – SPECIAL CONTRACT REQUIREMENTS

H014 SUCCESSOR CONTRACTOR (TAILORED)

(a)   This contract represents a continuing need of the Government, and as such, it is anticipated that, upon completion or termination of this contract, another contract for substantially the same effort will be executed. In the event that another Contractor is selected as the "successor" Contractor, it is mutually agreed and understood that the Government interests in such a case may be best served through employment by the successor Contractor of Contractor employees who may be acceptable to the successor Contractor and who otherwise elect to accept employment with the successor Contractor.

INTERPETATION: This is a standard clause on recurring contracts where government ensures a smooth transition of service from the incumbent to the new contractor by encouraging the new contractor to hire from the existing contractor staff.

8.3.10 SECTION I – CONTRACT CLAUSES

AIR FORCE FEDERAL ACQUISITION REGULATION SUPPLEMENT
5352.201-9101 OMBUDSMAN (TAILORED)
(a) An ombudsman has been appointed to hear and facilitate the resolution of concerns from offerors, potential offerors, and others for this acquisition. When requested, the ombudsman will maintain strict confidentiality as to the source of the concern. The existence of the ombudsman does not affect the authority of the program manager, contracting officer, or source selection official. Further, the ombudsman does not participate in the evaluation of proposals, the source selection process, or the adjudication of protests or formal contract disputes. The ombudsman may refer the party to another official who can resolve the concern.

INTERPETATION: This clause is commonplace on procurement actions having a high probability of *protest* by one or more contractors. The ombudsman is responsible for being the "first line of defense" representing government to diffuse possible contractor complaints or protests that are oftentimes the result of a misunderstanding by the contractor on how government conducts business. Note the ombudsman does not have any authority to make decisions on behalf of government or serve on the Source Selection Evaluation Board in any capacity.

8.3.11 SECTION K – REPRESENTATIONS, CERTIFICATIONS AND OTHER STATEMENTS OF OFFERORS

K003 CERTIFICATE OF SIGNATORY AUTHORITY

I, ___ (Name), certify that I am the ___ (Position Title) of the Corporation named as Contractor herein, that ___ (Name), who signed this contract on behalf of the Contractor, was then ___ (Position Title) of said Corporation; that said contract was duly signed for and on behalf of the said Corporation by authority of its governing body and is within the scope of its corporate powers.

(SEAL)   _____ (Signature)
                          _____ (Typed or printed Name and Title of Signatory)

INTERPETATION: This person has the authority to sign the SF33 as the company's representative. This person also typically represents the company in negotiations after proposal submission. If the contract is signed in a capacity other than principal, partner, or company officer, evidence of the signing authority must be furnished.

8.3.12 SECTION L – INSTRUCTIONS, CONDITIONS AND NOTICES TO OFFERORS

L014 SOLICITATION EXCEPTIONS

> Should the Offeror not concur with the proposed contract schedule and provisions, or desires modification thereto, it should be so stated in the proposal transmittal letter with reasons therefore.

INTERPETATION: Don't make the proposal evaluators read through half your proposal to determine you cannot support all mandatory requirements in the solicitation. Place a statement that you take no exception to the solicitations requirements in your cover letter transmitting your proposal to the client. Also, include a similar statement in the closing paragraph of your Executive Summary. If you do take exception to any requirements and provisions of the solicitation, include a statement in the transmittal letter explaining why. We'll look more closely at Section L requirements in Chapter 9 to follow.

8.3.13 SECTION L – INSTRUCTIONS, CONDITIONS AND NOTICES TO OFFERORS

L029 DETERMINATION OF COMPETITIVE RANGE (TAILORED)

> (a) Pursuant to FAR 15.306, the Source Selection Authority's (SSA) determination of a <u>competitive range</u> of proposals submitted as a result of this solicitation will consider such criteria as <u>technical evaluation/ranking of the proposal, initial cost/ price proposed, and other items set forth in Section M "Evaluation Criteria,"</u> of this solicitation.

> (b) Offerors are hereby advised that <u>only those proposals</u> <u>determined to have a reasonable chance for award of a contract will be</u> <u>included in the competitive range.</u>

INTERPRETATION: Based upon a review of each offeror's proposal, when compared to the Evaluation Criteria (Section M of the RFP), the Source Selection Authority (SSA) may eliminate one or more contractors from further consideration if they fall outside the Competitive Range. If this occurs you will be notified and given three-days to request a Preaward Debrief to help you understand why you did not make the Competitive Range. The Preaward Debrief is an important opportunity to learn what you can do next time to improve your proposal. The Preaward Debrief will be further described in Phase 3, Chapter 12.

STEP 4: Assess Competition

This step asks you to once again look at your competition now that you have the Final RFP in hand.

Draw from the SWOT and Competitive Analyses done in Phase 1 and Sections 5.1.1 and 7.3. Update as necessary for any changes in the RFP. These changes may lead you to conclude that your list of strengths and weaknesses may have changed or there are new requirements imbedded in the Final RFP that would give you a competitive advantage. Remember, these seemingly small changes (or possibly big ones) may change your WIN Theme.

STEP 5: Match RFP Key Requirements with Your Strengths and Weaknesses

At this time you should have a list of your company's strengths and weaknesses and a solution to include in your proposal to overcome past weaknesses from your WIN Theme Exercise in Table 11, Section 7.3. From this starting point you can now match your theme points with the RFP Requirements, and since you now have the Final RFP, you can easily see if there are holes in your proposal. A hole essentially means you have no key or subordinate theme points to address a requirement in the proposal. That's OK, it's still early enough in the process to continue filling the voids. Remember, a theme point may be a company strength or your solution to a company weakness.

For instance, if you have had problems on past and/or ongoing contracts, retaining high-caliber supervisory people, include a section in your proposal specifically addressing, "How we will attract and retain High-Quality Supervisory Talent." Or, if you've implemented a process to resolve chronic company problems then tell the proposal readers that you implemented a fix to the problem 12 months ago and comment on the positive results you've witnessed to date. Never leave it to the discretion of the reader to interpret what remedies, if any, have been implemented by your company to solve past problems.

STEP 6: Bid/No-Bid Decision

This is your final opportunity to choose to move forward; develop a proposal and involve others, or simply let this opportunity pass by. It is here where many companies go astray either by postponing their decision until the last minute, when they simply could not create a credible proposal, or moving forward to bid when gaping holes still remain in strategic issues. It is at this juncture where I see many companies not completing the match of their strengths and weaknesses, the proposal requirements and honestly assessing whether they have a chance of winning or not. It's simply a matter of forced issues; if your people are working on a proposal effort they cannot be working on something else. If you choose to proceed, this is when the proposal development will begin to cost Bid & Proposal (B&P) money and divert people from billable work. This is a critical decision.

STEP 7: Send No-Bid Letter

A No-Bid Letter is a simple one-page statement that you do not intend to bid this particular solicitation. You may or may not include an explanation, but it helps the government to know why you chose not to bid. If there are many such responses, the government may choose to make changes or amendments to the solicitation to foster increased competition. Such changes are commonplace when government did not issue a Draft RFP for industry to review.

It is not mandatory for you to send a no-bid letter to the government. If you should decline to bid you'll still be identified through CCR on similar, future opportunities as eligible to bid. This is sometimes not the case when doing business with national laboratories. As I mentioned in Section 3.5, the labs frequently rely on an in-house list of qualified vendors and suppliers when distributing a synopsis for a new contract. In this case, it's a requirement to send a no-bid letter to inform the lab of your desire to remain on their in-house list so you are notified of future opportunities in your area of expertise.

STEP 8: Finalize Your Team, Theme, and Schedule

Now that you're committed to bidding, let's proceed with this important step.

STEP 8-1: Finalize Team

You probably have always had an idea whom you would call upon for help as a Subject Matter Expert (SME). Now, with the schedule for proposal delivery staring at you, you can finalize your list of team members based upon the short-term workload, availability of specialists and information that already exists in your Resource Library.

Figure 16 shows the complete picture of what functions are necessary to move forward with the proposal effort. Be advised, in a small company, several functions are often performed by one person. This is where the handoff from the Business Development Manager to the Proposal Manager occurs. The BDM dealt with the strategic issues leading up to RFP receipt and the decision to Bid. Hereafter, the daily responsibilities will be handled through the Proposal Manager and his/her team. One notable exception is if you did not have the benefit of a Draft RFP or sufficient intelligence in Phase 1 to suggest your need for Strategic Suppliers or Teaming Partners. In this particular case, strategic issues will arise and continue to be the responsibility of the BDM. Other team members I did not discuss earlier, include your support functions personnel and Subject Matter Experts (SMEs).

Figure 16. Proposal Team

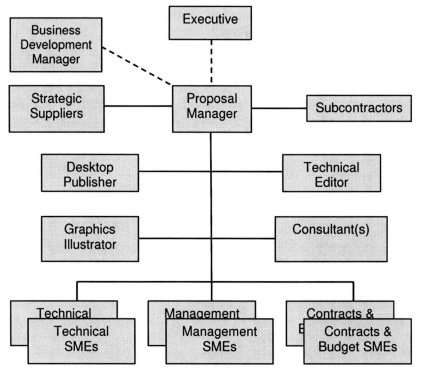

Through the company's strategic planning process, it is the *Executive* who helps identify and pursue emerging business opportunities. This is typically done through the priorities and commitment of resources he or she makes. The *Business Development Manager* (BDM) has the responsibility of translating the overall corporate business direction and limited resources into that next opportunity the company will bid. Many actions and decisions guide this important work.

The *Proposal Manager* is the tactical executioner receiving guidance from the BDM in the form of an Executive Summary and WIN-Theme to focus the proposal team from receipt of RFP through submission of your proposal. He/she formulates and submits questions from the RFP requiring clarification and represents the company, along with the BDM, when exchanging information and negotiating with government. It's commonplace for the proposal manager to become the Project or Program Manager for proposal efforts he/she had led.

There are no Strategic Suppliers in the BRASS example. Your *Teaming Partner* will likely serve as a subcontractor where you would dictate the organization of the proposal team and contributions of the sub. The roles of course are reversed when you become the sub and assume a subordinate role to the prime contractor.

Support functions include the *Desktop Publisher*, *Technical Editor*, *Graphics Illustrator*, and *Consultant* Support.

The importance of a proven *Graphics Illustrator* cannot be overstated. With limited guidance, this special individual possesses the ability to summarize pages of information in a handful of tables, charts, and graphs. This visual summary makes better use of limited writing space and is read twice as often at text.

For routine administrative actions, such as faxing or copying, proposal team members typically do it themselves in the interest of time. Most often, *Administrative Support* includes the desktop publishing and reproduction of the final products before shipping.

If you're fortunate to have a *Technical Editor*, this person will ensure a consistent ease of reading throughout the documents. This is especially important where there are many authors (SMEs) contributing to the proposal. Seemingly small inconsistencies in writing styles could cause Proposal Evaluators to lose their train of thought as they move through the pages of your proposal. If you don't have the benefit of a Technical Editor, make sure someone with an independent view of the final product reviews it before you go to press. This will be described in STEP 14; End-to-End Review. A review avoids one common complaint from government and lab Proposal Evaluators where many simple typos and grammatical errors could influence their impressions of the quality of your work.

Use of *Consultants* – When I was employed by that five-person engineering company right after college, if I needed the input of a specialist, that void was typically filled by my reading a book or searching the library that evening. Today we search the web and review our Library Resources. If that approach isn't enough, consultants can play an important role as technical specialists to the Proposal Manager as an integral part of the team, or as a passive contributor of a few pages to respond to a new requirement. I can recall one instance where I was hired to contribute a few pages of a proposal's quality section and quickly became the Proposal Manager when the company president became consumed in her divorce proceedings. In small companies, consultants can provide an indispensable service as a Red Team reviewer or as an independent third party to interview existing clients to assess your performance *before* it is documented as past performance, help position you for that next must-WIN contract, or a host of other services.

There are several kinds of *Subject Matter Experts* (SMEs) ranging from technical and management people who perform similar work for existing clients to *contracts* and *budget* people who play an important role in every proposal created by the company. The role of Contracts in your company can range from merely reviewing the RFPs clauses and making a determination of the company's ability to comply up to preparing Reps & Certs and representing the company in contract negotiations before award.

Budget or accounting staff generate cost estimates to help determine what the company could afford to spend in various cost categories to perform the work based upon a "cost bogie" provided by the BDM. Also, the accounting person must be involved with the evolving technical and management changes in the proposal that can impact pricing.

Today, with the advent of wireless laptops and Internet Cafes, the availability of a team member to support a proposal effort takes on new meaning. So many of the constraints that limited the use of specialists in the past have been overcome by technology using inexpensive web conferencing solutions to meet, coordinate, perform white-board exercises, and revise documents interactively. If fact, the Proposal Manager can accept sections for proofing and integration, chart daily progress, and perform white-board exercises through such a service. I personally use GotoMeeting.com for this purpose. We'll discuss the topic of staying on track further in Chapter 10.

STEP 8-2: Finalize Theme

Distribute a copy of the Executive Summary to your team and review the main points that will be included in the proposal. This may be the first opportunity for some to learn that, as the detailed proposal outline begins to take shape, it will be everyone's job to ensure the proposal theme is stated in the appropriate sections of the proposal outline. Solidifying your WIN Theme here provides everyone on the team a clear understanding of the precise words and phrases that need to be added into your proposal to convey the intended message.

STEP 8-3: Finalize Proposal Schedule

It has been said that the difference between a true project and a dream is a project schedule. It has also been said that proposals are never done, they're just due. So it's the Proposal Manager's responsibility to deliver a quality product, on time. Figure 17 summarizes a schedule to support a 30-day proposal delivery. Each of the 17 STEPs corresponds to the proposal development process flowchart I introduced in Section 8.2, Figure 13. Like an accordion, the schedule may be stretched for longer time periods, as in the case of a Research & Development (R&D) contract where you typically have a 6-week turn around. Or the schedule can be compressed if you have only two or three weeks to respond. As you can see, there are a lot of steps to be accomplished by a small core team in the early stages. This accelerated schedule in its first few days is designed to produce a definitive decision to bid, or not to bid. This leaves sufficient time to create and refine your proposal.

Figure 13. 30-Day Proposal Schedule

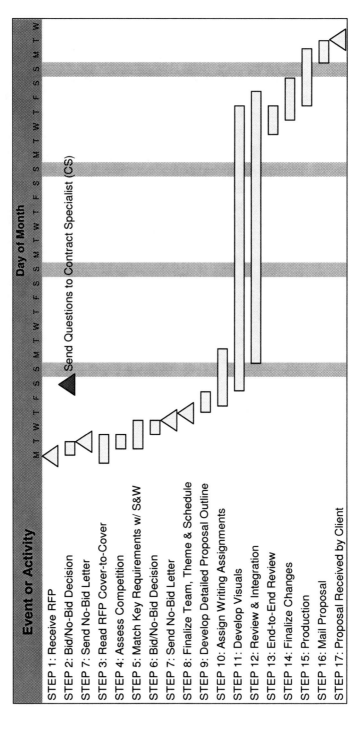

Beyond the steps already discussed, there are two more you should be aware of. In Figure 17 I have a milestone labeled "Questions Due to Contract Specialist (CS)." This date is specified in the RFP so you may receive a timely response that could influence your proposal. The second schedule item, which is not on the schedule, is legal review. If there are strategic suppliers or teaming partners you have not worked with before, having new agreements processed through legal review can be a lengthy, time-consuming, and iterative process.

Time to conduct an End-to-End Review is included in STEP 13. Frequently called the *Red Team Review*, this important step may take numerous forms. The purpose of the review is to ensure that someone (or a several people) verify that all of the requirements are sufficiently addressed throughout the proposal. In very small companies, fewer than 10 employees or so, they may perform a less rigorous approach to review for continuity of tough, and obvious errors. This very small company approach places a tremendous amount of responsibility on those developing the proposal detailed outline. Here, there will be no one to go back and independently review the tractability of RFP requirements through final proposal.

This concludes Chapter 8. In it I introduced the 17-Step Proposal Development Process and we began reviewing the first few steps. In Chapter 9 we'll continue Phase 2, Proposal Development, focusing on creating a detailed outline. This outline will serve as the focal point for satisfying all client requirements, adding in charts and graphs to enhance the delivery of your proposal, and provide the team with the tools to remain on track.

Chapter 9.0 Proposal Development
(Phase 2 Continued)

Chapter 9.0 will help you develop the organization, content, substance and substantiation that prove you are the one company best suited to deliver on this contract. Everything presented prior to this chapter has prepared you for Phase 2.

Proposal evaluators come from a wide variety of backgrounds. Therefore, it behooves you to write to many audiences. Also, to be responsive, you must respond to all of the requirements in the solicitation.

A well-developed proposal

- Ensures all requirements are met

- Ensures you can track requirements through the completed proposal

- Is easy to read

- Receives higher scores than less-organized proposals

The consequence of haste in the early stage is often a rough draft that requires more work to revise. Typically, this is not uncovered until it is too late in the timeline and there is no time to correct basic structural problems in the proposal. When I see a proposal team churning out work that has a logical place in the proposal, typically that means they invested heavily early on to develop a solid, detailed proposal outline. Conversely, if I observe a proposal team creating reams of paper and visuals with no clear place for them to go, chances are the Proposal Manager skipped this important step.

STEP-9: Develop Detailed Proposal Outline

Developing the detailed proposal outline includes eight parts as listed below:

STEP 9-1: Organize proposal volumes and top-level outline

STEP 9-2: Expand outline to reflect Evaluation Criteria

STEP 9-3: Integrate client vocabulary

STEP 9-4: Integrate WIN Theme

STEP 9-5: Brainstorm details beneath outline headings

STEP 9-6: Smooth outline

STEP 9-7: Allocate page count

STEP 9-8: Make a good proposal great

Let's begin.

STEP 9-1: Organize Proposal Volumes and Top-Level Outline

You begin by organizing the RFP requirements on the wall of your War Room as shown in Figure 18. With solicitations being delivered today via the internet in electronic form, it's easy to create Post-It note-type paragraphs, as shown in Figure 18, so you can begin *storyboarding* your proposal for easy reorganization of requirements, with your reply to follow in subsequent steps.

Figure 18. Starting to Organize Solicitation Requirements

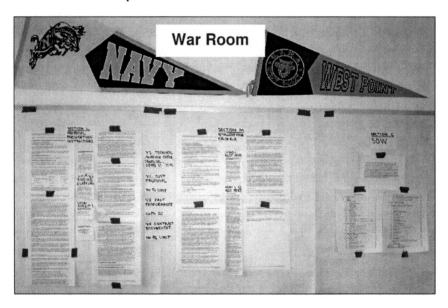

A storyboard is a graphical means of organizing your proposal and all of its contents. The process of visual thinking and planning allows a group of people to brainstorm together, placing their ideas on storyboards and then arranging the storyboards on the wall. This fosters more ideas and generates consensus inside the group. There are two advantage of using storyboards in developing a proposal outline:

1. It allows the team to experiment with changes in the flow of information to help Proposal Evaluators arrive at the conclusion you desire.

2. It allows you to easily move your response around when it appears to be asked for in more that one requirement. On the storyboard, you can easily "see" where you need a more detailed explanation of your approach with subsequent brief statements to reinforce what has already been said.

As you can see in Figure 19, you begin laying out the requirements for each main section of the solicitation on three storyboards; Section L: Proposal Preparation Instructions; Section M: Evaluation Criteria; and Section C: Statement of Work. Note that each requirement is "tagged" with the section and paragraph number it came from in the original requirement. This is your first step toward ensuring all solicitation requirements are addressed as you move forward.

Next, we expand the outline as specified in Section L, Proposal Preparation Instructions. An excerpt of this guidance is included below followed by my interpretation of how you might reply to this requirement.

L019 PROPOSAL PAGE LIMITATIONS AND NUMBER OF COPIES

a) The offeror's response to the requirements of this solicitation shall be contained in the <u>specific volumes identified below</u>. The number of copies and the maximum page limitations are provided. These <u>page limitations will be strictly enforced</u>. In the event an offeror exceeds the specified limit for the technical proposal, the <u>Government will not evaluate any pages in excess of the maximum</u>.

Vol.	Title	Number of Copies	Page Limitation
1.	Technical/Mission Capability Proposal	Original + 7	25 (single-spaced)
2.	Cost Proposal	Original + 8	None
3.	Past Performance	Original + 6	20 (double-spaced)
4.	Contract Documentation	Original + 1	None

INTERPRETATION: The guidance above establishes the overall structure of your proposal submission. It clearly states four separate volumes are required with an appropriate number of copies to support the government proposal evaluation team. Later guidance in Section L begins to identify the main headings of each volume. This information allows you to reorganize your Figure 15 storyboards into six detailed storyboards that begin to show the form and flow of your proposal submission.

Figure 19. Using Storyboards to Organize Proposal Volumes and Track Progress
(Page 1 of 2)

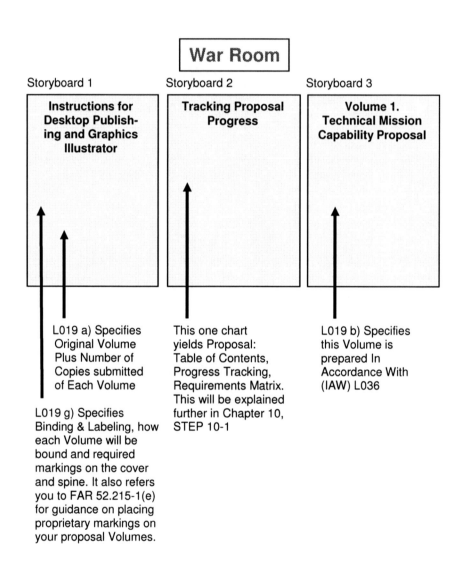

War Room

Storyboard 4	Storyboard 5	Storyboard 6
Volume 2. **Cost Proposal**	**Volume 3.** **Past Performance**	**Volume 4.** **Contract** **Documentation**

L019 c) Specifies this Volume is Prepared IAW L034

L019 d) Specifies this Volume is prepared IAW Past Performance Evaluation Criteria In Section M, Paragraph M002

L019 e) Specifies this Volume is organized IAW L019 e) to include 1) SF-33 with blocks 12-18 completed by the offeror, 2) RFP Sections B-J, 3) RFP Section K. etc.

In Figure 15 we can see that Storyboards 3 through 6 correspond to Section L guidance described above. Storyboards 1 and 2 are for our internal purposes. *Storyboard 1* is where you consolidate Section L guidance that is used by your Desktop Publisher and Graphics Illustrator. Such guidance, as shown in Figure 14, includes specifying the number of original volumes and copies that are submitted to the government. This allows the desktop publisher to begin setting up the overall structure of the proposal submission. Later, the number of copies is used to reproduce the proper numbers of copies for each Volume (L019 a)). L019 g) tells the graphics illustrator that the final proposal visuals: tables, charts and figures should have a minimum font size of 6 point (pt).

Storyboard 2 is used to organize the proposal submissions and track progress. It also creates the Table of Contents (TOC) and Requirements Matrix that will be submitted to the government as part of your proposal. The subject of Tracking Progress, the TOC, and Requirements Matrix are so important, I've dedicated Chapter 10, STEP 12-1 to expanding the idea of tracking progress.

Storyboard 3 is where you begin developing the detailed outline for Volume 1, Technical/Mission Capability Proposal. *Storyboards 4, 5 and 6* include the details for organizing Volumes 2, 3, and 4 respectively. Let's look at Storyboard 3 more closely.

Storyboard 3, Volume 1, guidance is provided in Section L, for Factor 2 as shown below.

L036 INSTRUCTIONS FOR PREPARING TECHNICAL PROPOSALS

(b) The Technical Proposal Volume should be specific and complete. Your responses will be evaluated against the mission capabilities factors defined in Section M. <u>All the requirements specified in this solicitation are mandatory</u>, however, of particular importance is your approach for conducting/providing services described below.

(1) Factor 2, Subfactor 1: Personnel Qualifications - Corporate Experience

    a.   Describe your organization specific to this acquisition
    b.   Describe the experience, expertise and qualifications of your key personnel
    c.   Describe the quality and relevancy of the offeror's corporate experience as it relates to the proposed effort

INTERPRETATION: L036 above describes the main headings government wants to see in your proposal. Upon opening your Volume 1 proposal for evaluation and scanning of your TOC, the government proposal evaluators will make their first judgment that "The contractor is well organized and this proposal will be easy to evaluate." or "Gee, this is going to be time consuming and painful!"

There is similar guidance in Section L to begin outlining Volumes 2, 3, and 4. Next, let's review how the Evaluation Criteria influences your detailed outline.

STEP 9-2: Expand Outline to Reflect Evaluation Criteria

This step integrates the Evaluation Criteria into Storyboards 3 – 6 to expand your outline. This approach ensures your proposal response will directly track the "scorecard" by which you will be evaluated. This makes it easy for the Evaluation Team members to find your reply in an easy-to-follow flow of information. Remember, the evaluators are human beings and not all of them are specialists on your subject or industry. This organization will make their job easier and, hence, earn you additional points. Conversely, the more difficult you make it for them to follow your proposal, the fewer points you will be awarded due to shear human error and oversight.

Below is an excerpt from the Evaluation Criteria, Section M, showing you how it influences the proposal outline and how your proposal will be graded.

M002 EVALUATION CRITERIA

a) Evaluation Factors and Subfactors and their Relative Order of Importance

Award will be made to the offeror proposing the combination most advantageous to the government based upon an integrated assessment of the evaluation factors and subfactors described below. Mission Capability and past performance are of equal importance and significantly more important than proposal risk and cost; however cost will contribute substantially to the selection decision. Within the Mission Capability factor, the subfactors are of equal importance.

    Factor 1: Past Performance
    Factor 2: Mission Capability
            Subfactor 1: Qualifications-Corporate Experience
            Subfactor 2: Management
    Factor 3: Price/Cost
    Factor 4: Proposal risk

INTERPRETATION: The first statement in Section M002; Evaluation Criteria, is consistent with what you read in any Best Value procurement, "Award will be made to the offeror proposing the combination most advantageous to the government." This allows the Source Selection Authority (SSA) and Source Selection Evaluation Board (SSEB) to make tradeoffs against Factors 1 through 4 above when choosing the contractor who will WIN contract award. Subjectively, the government reserves the right to make its award decision based upon an overall evaluation of Past Performance, Mission Capability, Price/Cost and Proposal Risk.

Let's review the influence of M002 as reflected in Figure 20.

Volume 1 is modified to reflect how it will be evaluated, and hence organized, in accordance with Factors 2 and 4. Factor 2 guidance calls for two main sections or headings in Volume 1 as shown below

- ## Qualifications-Corporate Experience (Subfactor 1)

- ## Management (Subfactor 2)

Factor 4 guidance, Proposal Risk, states Volume 1 will be evaluated at the Subfactor levels shown above. Therefore, Qualifications and Management each will be evaluated for the risks and a weakness associated with an offeror's proposed approach and includes an assessment of the potential for disruption of schedule, increased cost, degradation of performance, and the need for increased government oversight, as well as the likelihood of unsuccessful contract performance. For each risk identified by the government, the assessment also addresses the offeror's proposal for mitigating the risk and why that approach is or is not manageable.

Figure 20. Revising Storyboards to reflect M002 Guidance

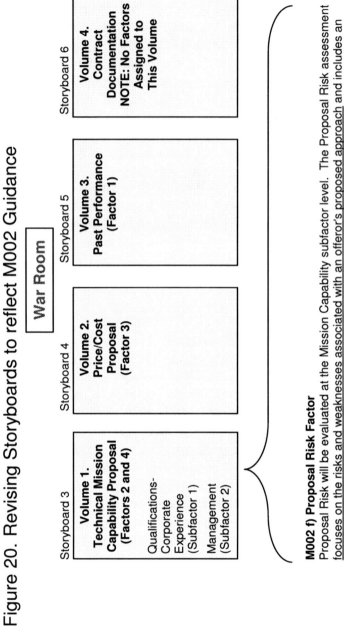

M002 f) Proposal Risk Factor

Proposal Risk will be evaluated at the Mission Capability subfactor level. The Proposal Risk assessment focuses on the risks and weaknesses associated with an offeror's proposed approach and includes an assessment of the potential for disruption of schedule, increased cost, degradation of performance, and the need for increased Government oversight, as well as the likelihood of unsuccessful contract performance. For each risk identified by the Government, the assessment also addresses the offeror's proposal for mitigating the risk and why that approach is or is not manageable. Each Mission Capability subfactor will receive one of the Proposed Risk ratings defined at AFFARS 5315.3 paragraph 5.5.2 Table 2, Proposal Risk Ratings.

Volume 2 is modified with Factor 3 guidance; hence the Volume title is changed to Price/Cost Proposal.

Volume 3 is influenced by Factor 1 guidance, with no detailed section headings being called out, but is "tagged" as being evaluated and hence IAW Factor 3 guidance.

Note there are no evaluation criteria for Volume 4. This volume contains Contract Documentation that is primarily a set of fill-in-the-blank forms completed by the contractor; SF33 with blocks 12-18 completed by the offeror, RFP Sections B-J with appropriate fill-in items completed, RFP Section K, Reps & Certs, etcetera (IAW L019 e).

Let's look at how a close review of what M002 adds to your main section headings in Volume 1 and expands the detailed outline for the Qualifications – Corporate Experience Section Heading

M002 EVALUATION CRITERIA

d) Mission Capability Factor

Each subfactor within Factor 2, Mission Capability Ratings, is <u>based on the assessed strengths and proposal weaknesses</u> of each offeror's proposal <u>as related to each of the Mission Capability subfactors</u>. The <u>evaluation</u> of Mission Capability will include <u>strengths, weaknesses and risks</u>.

(1) Qualifications - Corporate Experience will be evaluated to *determine how suited the offeror is to execute the contract.* Specifically, the <u>experience, expertise, and qualifications of the proposed key personnel relevant to the proposed efforts in the PWS;</u> and the <u>quantity and relevancy of the offeror's corporate experience as it relates to the proposed efforts. Failure to include a statement that all key personnel will be available in the event of a contract award or data showing that the offeror has obtained a commitment, letters of intent, or has a recruitment plan, may result in an unacceptable rating.</u>

(2) Management will be evaluated to determine the degree to which the offeror demonstrates the capability to effectively and efficiently manage the same or similar contract requirements. The following specific areas will be evaluated: initial staffing, personnel end

strength to include plans for maintaining adequate staffing for the life of the contract, staffing vacancy filling, and contract phase-in/transition.

(3) The technical proposal will be evaluated for source selection award purposes, based upon the technical proposal for the basic performance work statement. Proposals will be analyzed/evaluated in accordance with Section M evaluation criteria to ascertain who the contract winner will be.

INTERPRETATION: Your proposal will be assessed on its strengths, weaknesses, and risks compared to the Factors and Subfactors in Section M. Therefore, since you will be evaluated according to the main headings below, it behooves you to use similar phrases in the headings of the paragraphed sections of your proposal.

(1) Qualifications – Corporate Experience
(2) Management
(3) The Technical Proposal which will include your responses to the PWS

A further expansion of the outline is shown in Table 12 to demonstrate the direct correlation between what is called out in the Evaluation Criteria and how your detailed outline to the right ensures all requirements are addressed.

Table 12.   A Further Expansion of the Detailed Outline

M002 Guidance Directly Quoted from the Evaluation Criteria	Expansion of Proposal Outline IAW M002 Guidance
(1) Qualifications - Corporate Experience will be evaluated to *determine how suited the offeror is to execute the contract.* Specifically, the experience, expertise, and qualifications of the proposed key personnel relevant to the proposed efforts in the PWS; and the quantity and relevancy of the offeror's corporate experience as it relates to the proposed efforts. Failure to include a statement that all key personnel will be available in the event of a contract award or data showing that the offeror has obtained a commitment, letters of intent, or has a recruitment plan, may result in an unacceptable rating.	1) Qualifications – Corporate Experience • Our Highly Qualified Key Personnel • Experience, Expertise & Qualifications • INSERT Table summarizing quantity and relevance of experience to PWS • Assured Availability of Key Personnel • Our approach imposes Low-Risk to the Client • Highlight existing employees who will move to this contract • Refer to Letters of Intent in Attachment

STEP 9-3:   Integrate PWS Vocabulary

Integrating the client's vocabulary from their PWS into your outline is a large effort of "cut and paste." The source of this information is the Statement of Work (SOW), or in this case Performance Work Statement (PWS). The SOW/PWS is important because you need to demonstrate how you will accomplish all of the work, but it is not graded. Carefully read the SOW searching for key words and phrases that can be incorporated into the outline you just developed in 9-2 above. This process helps you to begin seeing how a detailed outline can be created and eventually serve as guidance to the Subject Matter Expert (SME) who will write the sections. Repetition of certain words or phrases in the PWS may provide valuable insight into what the customer feels is very important. Or it may highlight deficiencies in the existing contractor's work that the government wants to ensure is not overlooked in this new contract. Information extracted from the BRASS RFP below serves as one example of the kind of terminology you will need to integrate into your proposal. I chose this example because funds support and tracking is a routine government function.

EXERPT FROM BRASS DRAFT PWS

1.3.3 PROGRAM/PROJECT SUPPORT.
The contractor <u>shall</u> support divisions/branches/individual technical projects. Overall support of an effort includes, but is not limited to providing: program planning; program control support; <u>funding support and tracking</u>; schedule monitoring and reconciliation, computer support; facilities support; safety and security support.

1.3.3.3 Funding Support and Tracking.
The contractor shall:
- <u>Initiate the request for, and sign as requester on, funding documents for projects on contract and for any other contract items requiring additional funds.</u>
- <u>Support the project manager or project officer in the establishment, correction and completion of Job Order Numbers (JONs).</u>
- <u>Ensure that all levels of management have consistent and accurate financial information on assigned projects.</u>

INTEREPRETATION: There's a lot of verbiage in this example. In fact, this example was chosen from one of several PWSs you are required to bid. This one PWS is about 30 pages long, about the page count allotted for your entire Volume 1 submission. Therefore I quickly concluded that in the interest of space (if nothing else) I would not repeat a description of the PWS requirements. I concluded the explanation should include graphical explanations, possibly flowcharts, to describe how a company would perform all of the work embodied in the PWS without a lot of verbiage. I would also cite a procedures manual that would be used on a daily basis for the execution of routine work.

When adding PWS information to your storyboards you may interpret that it is appropriate to include the same information in more than one place in your proposal. Duplication is alright at this stage of outline development. The ultimate arbiter on how long a response you can submit will be determined by your page allocation.

STEP 9-4: Integrate WIN Theme

Next, integrate your WIN Theme into your outline. This information comes directly from the Chapter 7 exercise on theme development. In that exercise you learned that one theme point you're trying to make can really be placed into any number of sections of your proposal. For instance, *"We have lower project cost through innovation and safer solutions."* This brief statement would be appropriate for the introductory remarks of your Executive Summary or the summary paragraph of a main section of your proposal. In other places throughout your proposal you include the substantiating remarks for that one claim, *"We have lower project cost through innovation and safer solutions."* These substantiating remarks can appropriately go into the

- Management Section where you rely on small teams to brainstorm and recommend solutions that will both lower cost and enhance employee safety.

- In Past Performance you may include a statement where a similar participative management approach was employed successfully on an earlier contract.

- Furthermore, your Technical Process for accomplishing work is streamlined in the field where people who encounter problems have a proven method to involve others who could contribute to an innovative solution.

At this point you may believe you're simply capitalizing on your strengths. Nothing could be further from the truth. Your proposal is a plan of *how you will perform the work* if awarded the contract. So if your client has personal knowledge of your past shortfalls or it's documented in your Past Performance, remarks such as "your new approach to managing contract deliverables," or *"MyCompany's* approach to attracting, grooming, and retaining Project Managers for levels of increasing responsibility" can serve to answer questions concerning your past deficiencies. The challenge is to deliver on your promise when you WIN. This is also where you capitalize on the shortfalls of the incumbent or a competitor using techniques, such as ghosting, as described in Chapter 7. Here we:

- Reinforce your Strengths to Exploit Competitor Weaknesses.

- Focus on your Strengths you know your Competitor does not share.

STEP 9-5:   Brainstorm Details Beneath Outline Headings

Brainstorming is an effective way to generate multiple ideas on a specific issue and then determine which idea, or ideas, are the best. If participants feel free to relax and joke around, they'll expand their minds further and produce more creative ideas. A brainstorming session requires a facilitator, an uninterrupted space, and something on which to write ideas. The facilitator's responsibilities include guiding the session, encouraging participation and writing down ideas. Brainstorming is quite naturally applied to the proposal outline. The Proposal Manager is typically the facilitator on smaller proposals. You may also decide to call in a specialist to serve as the facilitator so the Proposal Manager may participate.

The focal point in these sessions is the storyboard you're focusing on at that moment. As you move from Storyboard 3, Volume 1, and continue down the wall, the group can make important decisions on where a theme point will merely be mentioned, or where it will be fully explained. The objective is to fill the voids in your proposal to offer detailed guidance to the SMEs who will write the sections. It is at this point where someone can speak up and say, "I have something that would work from a proposal I worked on last May," or "I just completed a final report for a contract that's wrapping up. It's got to be added to our Past Performance Volume."

STEP 9-6:   Smooth Outline

The flow of your proposal volumes is closely associated with readability and our notions of what "good" and "bad" writing is. A good flow to your proposal is the second indicator to the reader that yours is a "good" proposal.   The first indication is presentation: cover, format, use of visuals, use of color, etc.

Smoothing out the outline is a continuation of the creative process. Here you consolidate similar or redundant information, make decisions as to where theme points will be included as an explanatory paragraph or a brief sentence reinforcing a statement that had already been made, and apply editorial finesse.

Here we change passive statements made during a fast-paced brainstorming session into active voice. This is where you can write or rewrite *Action Captions* that grab the attention of the reader when they review your figures, tables, charts, and graph headings.

Smoothing the outline is an important step since this document will serve as your in-house "scorecard" to ensure all of the key points of your proposal are accounted for in the final proposal documents. This is an interactive process on the wall that refines what information will go where in the proposal to cast your company in the most favorable light.

The Front Matter is also accounted for and, at a minimum, includes a Title Page, Table of Contents, and Executive Summary.   The Executive Summary describes why *YourCompany* should be awarded the contract.   It summarizes all of the points you developed in your Proposal Strategy and initiates a standard approach used by all proposal contributors. The Executive Summary introduces the reader to the theme of your proposal. Later, the technical and management proposals reinforce the summary theme points. The proposal will close with a Summary of what you have just told the reader in your proposal, again reinforcing what was introduced in the Executive Summary and reiterated throughout. So by the time the proposal evaluator has completed reading the Summary, he or she should have heard an echo of your proposal strategy on at lease three occasions. What we were taught when first learning to write still holds true; tell the reader what you're going to tell them, tell them, and close with a reinforcing remark about what you just told them.

The iterative part is going back and forth between this step, and, Allocating Page Count, STEP 9-7.

STEP 9-7:   Allocate Page Count

Next, you can use an electronic spreadsheet, Microsoft Excel for instance, to determine the page count you will assign to each section including how much space you have for figures, tables, pictures, and other visuals and, of course, the written words. This allocation applies most often to the Technical and Management volumes of the proposal, wherever there is a limitation on the page count. But, the other sections of Budget, Certifications (Certs) and Representations (Reps) should also be accounted for when planning the ultimate reproduction and binding of the final volumes. This can impact the amount of consumables you use to complete the project.

Be advised that items in the appendix, such as resumes, sample materials, drawings, specification sheets, professional papers, capability statement, etc. are typically not included in your overall page count, but check Section L in your solicitation to make sure of the requirement.

If the page count and Section L instructions allow, the Executive Summary should be followed by a Requirements Matrix summarizing the proposal requirements and in which section of your proposal they are addressed. This important addition announces that you have met all of the Evaluation Criteria and

(SOW) requirements. It causes the proposal evaluator to breathe a sigh of relief knowing you have made their job easier and if they lose track while grading you, they can simply revert to this fold-out matrix. In those unusual instances where you do not meet non-mandatory or nice-to-have requirements, it tells the reader up front so they don't waste valuable time looking for your reply. This too means extra points!

STEP 9-8:   How to Make a Good Proposal Great

At this point you're probably breathing a sigh of relief that you're about to sit down and start writing. Writing constitutes a major milestone since most people consider it a measure of progress, to write *something*.

I suggest this is your last opportunity to take a final look at your storyboards and detailed outlines and ask the question, "What can we now do to embellish our proposal?"

Below I describe the four levels of a proposal; at each subsequent level you're delivering a message that increases your credibility. Moreover, you'll no doubt replace text with some kind of visual that will capture the readers' imagination to help them to "see" your credentials and the solution you're presenting.

Figure 17. The Four Levels to Making a Good Proposal Great

Increasing Proposal Quality →

Level 4: Benchmark

Level 3: Performance metrics

Level 2: Examples & anecdotes

Level 1: "Echo requirements"

LEVEL 1: "Echo requirements" - Probably the worst thing you can do when replying to an RFP is to simply echo back the requirement embodied in the SOW to the Proposal Evaluator. This level of response does not answer the basic question asked by the proposal evaluator, "how are you going to accomplish the work." This is also a common faux pas by the newcomer to proposal writing who has had little training or mentoring. Assuming we don't fit into that category, the lowest level of reply is to respond to the requirement by simply saying you have a successful method for accomplishing the work.

LEVEL 2: Examples and anecdotes - The next level of response says your company maintains a procedure or process for accomplishing this work. It also provides an example of how your company has successfully applied this approach in the past, which infers this approach would also be successful when applied to this new contract. This may be your first opportunity to use a visual. You can be sure an incumbent will use lots of photos of their employees working in the client's facility to add a sense of realism. You should show your people performing similar work to give the reader the impression, "We routinely perform this kind of work." Examples are beneficial to demonstrate Past Performance, for instance, your proven process that reflects seven years of improvements on similar contracts, etc. Flowcharts are often appropriate here to describe complex flows of work and information to reduce the amount of text.

LEVEL 3: Performance metrics - With Performance Based Service Contracts becoming so popular, we see metrics being used more and more to help quantify the performance of how you do business. This next level not only communicates that you have a process for accomplishing work, but you can quantify how well you do it through measurement. For example, a process that manages the receipt and expenditure of R&D funds may monitor when you've reached 80% of all available funds. This "trigger point" notifies the government person leading the R&D project to re-evaluate if there are sufficient funds to complete the work. This level of response states in quantifiable terms how well you do what you do and lends itself to graphics, including trend lines or bar charts, to demonstrate your performance, your grasp of the work, and its measurable outcomes. The measurements tell the government Project Manager how well the work performed by that process is proceeding. It can also help improve the process from one client to the next. It will help if the metrics you've measured before are the same, similar or easily adaptable to what's being requested in the quality requirements of this solicitation. You may always suggest metrics. If you're going to be measured by them, it helps to influence how you will be "graded."

LEVEL 4: Benchmark - Lastly, the final level demonstrates your success in accomplishing this work through measurement, and shows you have some notoriety in your field where you're the benchmark who leads the industry. This can be done by quoting accolades from clients, recognition through client award programs, or industry recognition through local or national awards. International Standards Organization (ISO) or Malcolm Baldrige National Quality Award recognition also serves as a benchmark-type of recognition because few can attain such a level without demonstrated results and client feedback.

Your proposal should demonstrate that you are at a Level 3 or 4 for all volumes. It is anticipated that the content of your reply will be minimally at Level 2 or 3 for areas you consider to be your strengths. These strengths will have surfaced in the development of your WIN Theme in Section 7.3.

In Chapter 9 we reviewed how to develop and refine your detailed proposal outline. This was the second chapter dedicated to Phase 2, Proposal Development. Chapter 10 will conclude proposal development. We will begin with STEP 10, Assign Writing Assignments, and conclude Phase 2 where the Proposal Manager verifies that your proposal masterpiece has been received by the client.

Chapter 10.0 Proposal Development (Continued)

Chapter 10 will cover the balance of the steps in Phase 2, Proposal Development. It begins after completing the detailed proposal outline with making writing assignments and ends when the Proposal Manager has verified the proposal has been received by the client.

STEP 10: Assign Writing Assignments

It's now time to meet with your entire team to give out writing assignments. Many have already been involved in developing the detailed outline, while others, for numerous reasons, are only available to simply receive your guidance and write their section for the proposal. An SMEs reply may be, "Gee, I can pull that from this other proposal" or "I'm going to need these other two people to get involved so I can assemble the appropriate data," or in the best case they say, "I know where I can find that information in our Resource Library and draft that section with little additional work."

Although you have a page count allocated for every section you're asking for, use this as a guide. It's much easier to edit down than to create additional information to fill the space. A good rule of thumb is to get 1 or 2 times the volume of words that was requested to fill the space. Instead of asking the SMEs to create and submit a perfect product, assume it will be rewritten. Therefore it is far more important to receive their rough input as soon as possible so you have more precious time to rework their input into the final product. Rewriting is also more important than writing because the proposal evaluators will be presented with a single writing style that will better allow them to follow your train of thought. A tool used to track progress is described below.

STEP 10-1: Tracking Proposal Progress

Delivering, in this case, a four-volume proposal in a few short weeks is a monumental task. Therefore, it behooves you to be as organized as possible so the entire team can visibly "see" progress. The approach I'll describe follows through with your objective to ensure all requirements are addressed. It also allows you to keep track of proposal inputs as it is received and accepted by the Proposal Manager.

This important work is tracked using an electronic spreadsheet as shown in Table 13. In this case I used a Microsoft Excel spreadsheet. The spreadsheet is organized in eight columns: Proposal Volume/Section/Paragraph (Column 1) through a series of "check" or "date postings" to identify when the sections, including charts & graphs, are received by the Proposal Manager and accepted (Column 8). Acceptance means the Proposal Manager reviewed an SMEs input against the detailed outline to confirm all of the main points are addressed and that there is more rather than less input, so it can be "edited down" to fit the allocated page count.

Note the question marks in Section 3.5, Basic PWS. Here, my first review of the solicitation was not clear and this reminds me to re-read and discuss with the rest of the team.

There are three uses for this spreadsheet:

- Track Proposal Progress
- Requirements Matrix
- Table of Contents

Table 13. Tracking Proposal Progress

Column 1	Column 2	Column 3	Column 4	Column 5	Col. 6	Col. 7	Col. 8
Proposal Volume/Section/Paragraph	Solicitation Requirement	Evaluation Factor, Section/Paragraph	Page Allocation	Writing Assigned To	DRAFT Due	DRAFT Charts & Graphs Due	Section Review & Integrated
Volume 1. Technical/Mission Capability Proposal	L036 (a)	M002 Factor 2					
Title Page							
Table of Contents							
List of Tables and Graphs	L019 (l)						
Glossary							
SECTION 1. Executive Summary							
1.1 Introduction	L014						
SECTION 2. Personnel Qualifications - Corporate Experience [Factor 2, Subfactor 1]		M002 Factor 2, Subfactor 1					
2.1 Our Organization to Support this Contract	L036 (b)	M002 Factor 2, Subfactor 1					
2.2 Our Experience, Expertise and Qualifications	L036 (b)	M002 Factor 2, Subfactor 1					
2.3 Quality and Relevance of our Teams Experience as it applies to this Procurement	L036 (b)	M002 Factor 2, Subfactor 1					
SECTION 3. Management [Factor 2, Subfactor 2]	L036 (b)	M002 Factor 2, Subfactor 2					
3.1 Initial Staffing	L036 (b)	M002 Factor 2, Subfactor 2					
3.2 Personnel End Strength	L036 (b)	M002 Factor 2, Subfactor 2					
3.3 Staffing Vacancy Filling	L036 (b)	M002 Factor 2, Subfactor 2					
3.4 Quality Control Plan	L036 (b)	M002 Factor 2, Subfactor 2					
3.5 Basic Performance Work Statement (PWS)	??????????						
3.6 Phase - In Transition Plan	L036 (b)	M002 Factor 2, Subfactor 2					
Volume 2. Cost Proposal	L034	M002 Factor 3					
Volume 3. Past Performance	L019 d)	M002 Factor 1.					
Volume 4. Contract Documentation	L019 e)						

Tracking Proposal Progress relies on all eight columns. Column 1 lists the sections of each proposal volume based upon Sections L, and M as used in Chapter 9. Although Table 13 is an abbreviated length of this work, it does show that you track progress down to the individual section level, where there's a paragraph heading of some kind. Columns 2 and 3 track the requirements that are addressed in each section. This is easy to accomplish using storyboard techniques and by *tagging* each requirement from its source in the solicitation. Here, all Section L and M requirements should be accounted for. For Column 4, Page Allocation, make sure that the maximum number of pages does not exceed those allowed in Section L of the RFP and any later amendments thereto. Columns 4 through 7 assign the writing and creation of charts and graphs to the appropriate person with a due date.

In the first few rows of Table 13 I listed 'Front Matter' that includes a Title Page and Table of Contents, list of Tables and Graphs, glossary of terms, and then Executive Summary at the beginning of Section 1. The Executive Summary is the second opportunity for the proposal evaluator to read why *YourCompany* should be awarded the contract and summarizes all of the points you developed in your WIN Theme. This subject will be briefly introduced in the cover letter transmitting your proposal to the client. Later, the Technical and Management Proposals reinforce these key points. The proposal will close with a Summary of what you have just told the reader in your proposal, again reinforcing what was introduced in the Executive Summary and reinforced throughout. So, by the time the proposal evaluator has completed reading the Summary, he or she should have heard an echo of your proposal theme on at lease four occasions; cover letter, Executive Summary, Technical and Management Sections of the proposal, and in summary remarks wrapping up a section. As we learned in grade school, tell the reader what you're going to tell them, tell them, and then tell them what you just told them.

If the page count and Section L instructions allow, the Executive Summary should be followed by a *Requirements Matrix* summarizing the proposal requirements and your ability to meet or exceed the requirements and what page delivers your reply. The Requirements Matrix (or Compliance Matrix as it is frequently called) is included in Section 1.3, at the end of the Executive Summary Section. This important addition sets the stage up front that you have met all of the Proposal Preparation Instructions (Section L) and Evaluation Criteria (Section M) requirements. It causes the proposal evaluator to breathe a sigh of relief knowing you have made their job easier and if they lose track of where they are grading you, they can simply revert to this matrix. Oftentimes, the requirements matrix is a fold-out on an 11-by-17 inch piece of paper so the evaluators can easily remove it and place it on the table in front of them for quick reference. In those instances where Section L does not request a requirements matrix, I recommend that, if you deem your proposal to be complex rather than simple and straightforward, in the interest of space, include it as an attachment so you don't use up valuable counted pages. Again, refer to Section L to confirm which Attachments are not considered in the page count.

This detailed outline will also serve as a "checklist" used by your Proposal Manager or Red Team to ensure all of the client's requirements are accounted for. As such, it provides an invaluable Quality Assurance role in completing the proposal.

The *Table of Contents* (TOC) for your proposal is also included in Table 13. Column 1, plus the section page number becomes your TOC.

So, this one table serves many purposes and saves valuable time. It is displayed on the wall during each meeting with your team to review progress. I prefer to hold my review meetings at the end of the day so anyone who is behind will have the evening to catch up so yet another day of "prime time," between 8 a.m. and 5 p.m. is not lost. This tool can also be reviewed over the internet if one or more of your team members is traveling.

STEP 11: Develop Visuals

"Common Sense tells us that a picture is worth a thousand words. The dilemma then becomes choosing the right picture to represent the right words."

Colleen Jolly, Principal
24 Hour Company

Proposal reading is tedious work. By the 3rd or 4th proposal the evaluators are tired, bored and finding it hard to follow the text. Visuals release the tension and make it easier to convey complex ideas that are reinforced by the accompanying text. Visuals also make your proposal much easier to understand because they distill complex information into a digestible presentation that will WOW the client! It links our emotions to a visual that influences the decision-maker. Visuals are also read twice as often as the text and are understood more than 60,000 times faster than text alone based upon research at 3M Corp. Well-organized and designed visuals displace more than the space they use, making it easier for the reader to understand and digest complex ideas. It also makes it easier to write to the illustrations because it is simpler to explain with fewer words. Fewer words are always better.

Informative and communicative design improves comprehension and retention of data and concepts. Visuals, if done properly, significantly increase the likelihood the client will agree with your concepts, leading to a decision to buy your solution over a competitors. When creating a visual for your proposal, the typical constraints are first time, and then money.

The following figures show some examples of professionally developed visuals and are accompanied by ideas of how they might be used in your proposal.

Figure 21. Proposal Volume Cover

Applications: When a small company takes its first leap to the next level in proposal design, they turn first to enhancing their visuals. If the budget is tight they may be inclined to invest in the proposal cover first. When proposal evaluators are first organized to begin the proposal evaluation, there's a 50-50 chance that they will be allowed to "grab" whichever proposal they choose first. If your cover and spine are attractive, professional and present a theme that resonates with the evaluator, they'll reach for that proposal first. Being first provides you with the opportunity to establish the standards by which every following proposal will be judged. It's a good investment.

Figure 22. Process Flow Chart

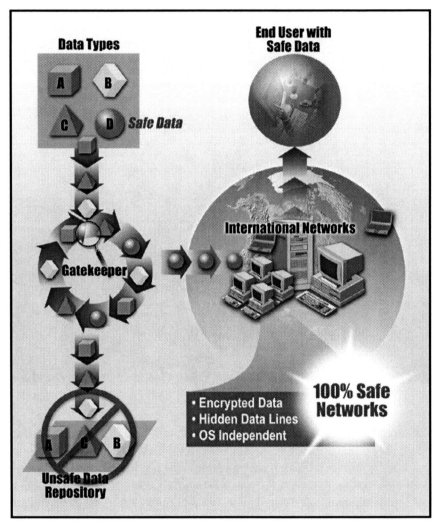

Applications: Figure 22 is one example of a *notional* flow chart beginning with input data and ending with "safe" data delivered to end users. Figure 13 is yet another example of a flow chart I used to introduce or "show" my 17-Step Proposal Development process. Flow charts are an invaluable tool to describe your work processes. Little narrative is required to explain them and the visual also creates a focus for the reader. Whenever a solicitation asks such questions as; "How will you ensure all design requirements will be accounted for?", "How will your approach ensure a high quality of service delivery in accordance without rigorous performance-based requirements?", or "What's your process to attract and retain highly qualified personnel to ramp up staffing to meet the demands of our new program?" Your answer to all of these questions should involve the use of process flow charts. It allows you to succinctly send the message that you have a proven, time-tested approach to

Figure 23. Pie Chart

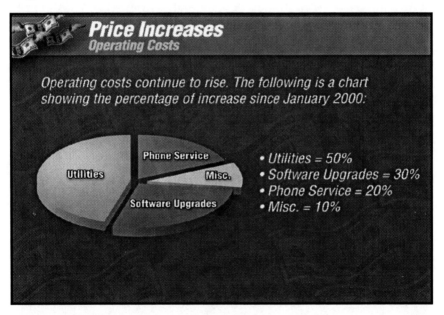

accomplish work with the necessary client interactions, design reviews and quality control checks planned and accounted for in your disciplined approach. A flow chart replaces tedious text and lends itself to giving the client anticipation that there is a detailed procedure manual behind the process. Flow charts are great communication tools.

Applications: Pie charts are a flexible way to show how all of the parts of a process or project come together to deliver a specific message. The sort of messages that can be easily conveyed using pie charts include; what percentage of Ph.D.'s, Masters Level, Bachelors-Level and trade school graduates will be brought to this important project; as in Figure 23 above, how are all of the costs allocated among the cost categories being tracked in the program; the distribution of experience levels of your people; the certifications of your trades people that will work on this high-priority program; and many others.

Figure 24. Conceptual Layout

Copyright 2007 ©, 24 Hour Company

Applications: The Conceptual Layout, shown in Figure 24, may be used to "show" the evaluator the layout of a new facility, describe how work flow will fit into the allotted floor space, etc. This figure makes the facility "look real"—more achievable and farther along than other offerors.

Below are some pointers to help make the most of your investment in visuals:

Templates - Establish templates in the early stages to ensure a standard format for your technical and management proposals, price/cost and other volumes, briefing charts, and file management. This not only improves the quality of your final product, but also saves costs and irreplaceable time in the process.

Logging graphics – *YourCompany* should have a numbering scheme in place to readily find and track charts, tables, and photographs in your Resource Library for immediate search and retrieval. This is essential for streamlining the production and design process and maintaining version control. One numbering scheme is XYZ_004V4, where "XYZ" is the name of the proposal or internal tracking, "004" is the assigned and never duplicated number and "v4" indicates the visual is on its fourth revision cycle. Numbering typically provides some indication of what proposal the visual is from along with the date of its last revision,

Bullets - Use bullets to ease reading by the evaluators and lessen the need to hunt for important information.

Icons – Include a handful of simple images to represent your solution or project to highlight innovations, best practices, cost benefits – anything your reviewer might find helpful that make a statement at a mere glance. Establish your icons early and stick to them! Any change in the icon usage/visuals may signal a change in meaning to your reader.

Graphics Production Time Estimates – This is the time it takes to create a visual, generally estimated at 4 hours, including a moderate number of iterations and aggregated over an entire proposal full of visuals. A good rule of thumb is listed below, but can be reduced by previously agreed upon standardized templates and by having all your information finalized before starting graphic development:

- Basic map chart or pie chart: 1-3 Hours

- Detailed stacked information, charts over screened images, cutaways of equipment, lengthy or data-rich matrices or tables: 3-8 Hours

- Photographic Montages, Photo Editing for background or color correction, 3-D illustrations of equipment or structures: 4-16 Hours (or more)

Because of the impact you can deliver through Proposal Graphics, it is typically one of the first outsourced functions for the following reasons:

- In-house work conflicts

- The "strategicness" of the bid

- Size of the bid (typically outsourced where bids exceed $10M/year in work)

- Proposal schedule conflicts with major holidays where it would be difficult to secure time commitments from support personnel during planned family time

- Limited proficiency of in-house skills

Graphics is one of the first proposal functions outsourced. Get these specialists involved in the project early on. Graphics people can help solidify WIN themes and offer a "god's eye" overview early in the process so all the authors have a common vision to write to. If budget is an issue, you can gang all the edits together. So, instead of running your organizational chart through Graphics when you have only 5% of the names, wait until you have 95%.

This section was prepared with the assistance of Colleen Jolly, a Principal of 24 Hour Company, a professional proposal graphics and production company. 24 Hour Company hires people who have the personality and energy to fit into the company culture, work side by side with client teams and learn the 24 Hour Company Success Formula to meet their proven 100% delivery standards.

Some of their clients are Northrop Grumman, Raytheon, L^3, ManTech, CSC, General Dynamics, and many others.

For more information:

Colleen Jolly, Principal
24 Hour Company
...bid-winning proposal graphics
6521 Arlington Blvd, Suite 501, Falls Church, VA 22042
colleen@24hrco.com
Phone: (703) 533-7209 FAX: (703) 533-3959
Website: www.24hrco.com

STEP 12: Review & Integration

Review and integration of proposal inputs is a lot like being a CPA at tax time. There isn't a lot of time for idle conversation.

The Proposal Manager serves as the single clearing house for all proposal inputs. He/she then performs three reviews after receiving an input. They are:

- Content

- Page count

- Consideration of any additional explanations, examples, quantifications or visuals that improve the input

The *first review* compares the detailed outline assigned to the SME and ensures that all of the points are addressed in the input provided to the Proposal Manager. Secondly, the PM verifies that the input is at least as long as required based upon the page allocation done in Table 13. Lastly, a decision is made on whether or not anything can be done to improve the quality of the input. In other words, can anything be done to "take this Section to the next Level," as described in Chapter 9, STEP 9-8 using relevant examples, photographs, tables, charts and graphs, etcetera. If additional data are required, or a trend chart needs to be prepared, make certain it's assigned to the SME or Graphics Illustrator to guarantee this action item is being worked.

On occasion, the due date and time comes and goes and no input was received for a critical section of the proposal. I've already explained what you can do to ensure the proposal team is armed with all of the information you have at your disposal to begin writing their assigned sections. Over time, you'll discover who you can rely on to deliver timely inputs while others seldom or never meet the suspense date. I've learned to deal with such setbacks proactively. I simply take the detailed outline and interview the SME to obtain the necessary narrative. We discuss other needed inputs such as data, diagrams, photographs, etc., to complete the transfer of information so the Proposal Manager can remain on schedule.

If you have access to an editor or technical writer, you may turn over the information to them for integration into the flow of the planned proposal volumes. Remember, anything you can do to smooth the input before it becomes part of your proposal, the greater the time savings when you perform your End-to-End Review. This will be discussed in STEP 13 below.

Lastly, update Table 13 to accurately determine the status of the proposal effort.

STEP 13: End to End Review

By this time proposal inputs have undergone review by the Proposal Manager before acceptance to ensure all of the points in the detailed have been addresses. A second review is performed by the Technical Editor for grammar, spelling, punctuation, and ease of reading including rewrites. This final review, called the *Red Team Review*, ensures all of the requirements in the solicitation have been met. It's not uncommon for large companies pursuing $100 million and multi-billion dollar contracts to conduct the Red Team review half-way through their proposal schedule. They anticipate major rewrites and changes in the structure of their response. In our case we budgeted a modest period of time and assume the team who created the detailed outline performed a thorough job.

The intent of your Red Team review is to have an independent pair of eyes take a fresh look at your proposal beginning with the solicitation. This review accomplished the following:

- Have all of the solicitation requirements been addressed

- Does the proposal flow where any proposal evaluator would easily follow your train of thought

- Does the presence of your theme lead the reader to your conclusion

STEP 14. Finalize Changes

Now all of the changes are made in the proposal documents and verified by the Proposal Manager and editor before producing all of the copies and originals for your submission as called for in Section L, Proposal Preparation Instructions.

STEP 15. Production

Production refers to all of the coordination, reproduction, and packaging to create the physical proposal, including the appropriate number of copies, hard-copy format and electronic. Some requirements call for producing proposals that will lie flat when read. Unless Section L specifically limits you, always try to deliver a proposal that will lie flat for the convenience of the proposal reader.

The production process represents an important milestone integral to the success of your proposal and at par with other milestones in the schedule. Respect the people who will be doing this important work. Some proposal production pointers you should keep in mind when going into production are

- There is no such thing as a *Standard Proposal,* each has its own special provisions that make it unique.

- The author may have crafted a brilliant 2-page section with a sketch of a ¼ page visual, but while the beautifully crafted visual was in final production, the size of the visual grew from ¼ page to ½ due to limitations in the smallest font size you could use according to Section L instructions.

- Microsoft Word and PowerPoint are fine for bidding a few million dollars a year in work. Beyond that you may need to move to more sophisticated desktop publishing software such as Adobe PageMaker, Adobe In Design or Quark Xpress. A good guide is Section L of the solicitation. If they ask for your electronic volumes to be submitted in Word, that may dictate your "preferred" software for that offer.

- Cross-referencing tools add tremendous convenience for creating a Requirements Matrix. The value in using these tools is not to create a professional looking table, that's the easy part; the advantage is the flexibility to instantaneously recreate the requirements matrix after last minute changes have been made to the proposal.

- Establish templates early on. Produce standard templates that are routinely used in all your submissions to the government: monthly progress reports, final reports, and the like.

- There is an absolute *"Print Time"* that needs to be acknowledged by the team.

- Backup often. With the advent of Flash Drives (or Jump Drives) backing up important information is easier than ever.

- Establish reliable and secure communication practices immediately, making sure this subject is covered during the kick-off meeting with your proposal team and in one-on-one sessions when SMEs are assigned work.

- Generally, copyright laws apply to most artwork. An image in a magazine is the property of the magazine. Your completed proposal will include markings that denote the proprietary nature of its content.

"Rapid turnaround is a myth in today's complex world where proposal deliverables include a myriad of book, presentation and electronic media."

Suzanne Kelman
Proposal Publishing Manager

Some tips to reduce proposal costs are listed below

1. Successive proposal drafts typically increase quality. Unnecessary iterations add time and cost.

2. Keep your team small. Large numbers of contributors add cost and slow the process.

3. Train your staff in advance of RFP receipt. Try to learn as much as you can and do as much as you can in advance of RFP release so everyone on your team understands their roles and responsibilities.

4. Form a team as early as possible and maintain team integrity throughout the process. Swapping

people adds to the confusion, reduces quality, and dilutes individual responsibility.

5. Maintain the schedule by conducting daily progress meetings and holding people accountable for deliverables.

6. Don't change review dates simply because "things aren't working out." Proposal development is an evolutionary process, you never "finish," you just run out of time.

7. Use valuable time before RFP release to organize yourself. Even before a DRAFT RFP release you know you will be asked (1) who will be involved in the project (organizational chart), (2) what you will do to accomplish the work (process), (3) when will you do the work (turn around times to support new and emerging work or Delivery Orders), where will the work be accomplished (layout; square-footage; address where work will be performed; specialized equipment, etc.) and how will you ramp up to begin work. This information should reside in your library in advance of receiving the RFP.

8. Establish a format for your resumes and tailor your resumes to the DRAFT RFP requirements. Ensure you have a matrix correlating RFP requirements to personnel skills.

9. Update you information on the Central Contractor Registration (CCR) database to reflect the authorized parties who will speak on behalf of your company.

10. Carefully target your "must-WIN" RFPs that are consistent with your company's strategic direction.

Start early and budget your resources necessary to WIN.

11. Centrally locate your proposal effort to maximize communication and minimize searching for people and paper.

12. Ensure security and information backups are available for anyone desiring to work at odd hours.

13. Stick with the schedule to remain on track and reserve the time at the end for a complete review.

Adapted from *Tips to Cutting Proposal Costs* by Duane Turnbull, APMP Journal Spring 2001.

STEP 16. Mail Proposal

There are a couple of points that should be mentioned here to ensure your proposal arrives on time.

You may need *redundancy in delivery methods* that would require producing two entire sets of deliverables. Plan to ship one and hand deliver the second.

Pay attention to the minutest details so your proposal arrives on time. I can think of one occasion where a colleague experienced delivering a proposal late to the client simply because the overnight delivery service was quoting a delivery time in his local time. Unfortunately, the proposal was headed east, three time zones ahead. Section A, the SF33 of the RFP specified the date and time the proposal was due to the government mailroom and of course, you guessed it, the package arrived late in the receiving time zone. It's sad to say since the proposal arrived late it was not considered. Also, on one occasion in my own career, I had to board a plane and personally delivered a proposal to MIT Lincoln Laboratories to ensure it arrived on time. A costly trip to be sure, but I did guarantee to my boss that our work made it into the client's hands on time.

STEP 17. Proposal Received by Customer

This is the last step in Phase 2. It requires the Proposal Manager to have some form of written acknowledgement that the proposal has arrived on time. This acknowledgement may take the form of a receipt from the Mail Room clerk or an email from the Contract Specialist (CS) who is logging in all of the proposal submissions on the day of arrival.

10.1 Oral Proposals

This Chapter would be incomplete if I did not include something on the important and timely subject of Oral Proposals. Across all agencies of the Federal Government, Oral Proposals are used 50% of the time. Below are some pointers to observe:

- Unless otherwise stated in Section L, organize your presentation in the same manner you created your detailed outline in Chapter 9.

- Intelligence from government PMs, CORs, COs, and CSs will tell you who should deliver your oral proposal. Some may prefer the marketing manager, while others prefer the president of the company to deliver opening remarks and introductions of the people who will actually perform the work delivering their area of specialization. This second approach provides an opportunity for the evaluators to "warm up" to your SMEs before the Question and Answer session begins.

- Practice your presentation so you can successfully cover all points within the allotted time.

- Anticipate questions and practice answering them.

- Within DOD it is typically a "supplement," in addition to the written volumes.

- Within the national labs, Oral Proposals are typically a replacement for the written proposal and in other instances they are "the next step" after you have made "the first cut and short list" in the Proposal Evaluation process.

- Knowledge of the presentation facilities, including room size, audio-visual support, and overhead and rear-projection capabilities is helpful to put you at ease in this new environment.

- Oral presentation slides must comply with response format instructions in Section L. The presentation template should be functional and have a corresponding appearance to the printed proposal.

- Typically delivery of the printed and electronic orals proposals coincides with delivery of the written proposals. This creates an extra workload for production.

- The most strenuous situation for your proposal team and the production people may occur when only offerors who make the "short list" are required to return to deliver their oral proposals. In this instance, the timing involved probably will dictate you work diligently on your oral proposal in advance of knowing whether you will present or not. This approach, while risky, ensures you have sufficient time to polish the handout materials and practice the presentation.

This concludes Phase 2, Proposal Development. In Chapter 11 we'll describe what occurs within government when your proposal is evaluated and how the Source Selection Authority (SSA) makes the decision on who will be awarded the contract.

Chapter 11.0 Government Proposal Evaluation

The steps in Chapters 5 through 10 were executed by your company leading up to submitting a WINning proposal. After proposal submission, the tempo of your work subsides, but work still remains. Essentially, you'll respond to the actions initiated by government while they evaluate your proposal. In this chapter you'll see a glimpse of what occurs within government after you've submitted your proposal. Armed with this knowledge, you may tweak future proposals. Also, you can anticipate your interactions with government so you will be better prepared.

In Chapter 11 we'll review the following three steps:

    STEP 1: Government Team Training
    STEP 2: Proposal Evaluation
    STEP 3: Contract Award

Let's look at each step more closely.

STEP 1: Government Team Training

The government team is trained in preparation for evaluating your proposal. If your product or service lends itself to a Small City contract, the training is probably minimal in that Contracts People perform this kind of review all of the time and are proficient. This is not the case for contracts for products and services that support

Core Functions, or require technical oversight of the contract work after award. These are the exceptions I described in Section 2.4 and apply to contracts managed through Civil Engineering, Environmental or Base Information Technology (IT) Office. In this case, the contract may support everyone on base (a Small City), but because of the technical nature of the work, daily management is conducted by the cognizant office who initiated the contract and manages the work. So, if your contract requires technical oversight, the people who will evaluate your proposal may not do this very often. Therefore, they are trained on their roles and responsibilities to fairly evaluate your submission against the Evaluation Criteria.

So the people who will receive this training consist of members of the Source Selection Evaluation Board (SSEB) and possible the Source Selection Authority (SSA). The SSEB is comprised of the people who will evaluate your proposal in the areas or main sections of the Evaluation Criteria from Section M. In the case of the BRASS contract, the volumes to be evaluated include Technical/Management, Price/Cost, Past Performance and Proposal Documentation.

STEP 2: Proposal Evaluation

One example of a Federal Government proposal Evaluation Process is depicted in Figure 25. This process applies for review of all four volumes of your proposal submitted to the government. Because of its importance, Past Performance is discussed separately in STEP 2-2. Although there is a lot of information on this chart, there are a few basic points I want to make. First, while government is evaluating your proposal, they summarize your proposal's strengths and weaknesses. Any need to clarify your proposal may be written up in Evaluation Notices or ENs according to the FAR. The second point is that these ENs may ask small, clarifying questions whereby after the proposal evaluators read your reply they may choose to take a downward path to Brief the SSA and swiftly move toward contract award without discussions or negotiations. This can result in contract award in a couple months rather than several months. In BLOCK 12 of the SF33 you signed and submit with your proposal, you were asked to acknowledge how long your proposal is good for. If government requests your offer be good for 120 days, this should indicate they may anticipate delays in getting the contract to award quickly. One factor that could stretch out this timeline is the upward path in Figure 25 is where the magnitude of the ENs government asks you to reply to require discussions and a re-evaluation of your proposal. More information on government's proposal evaluation is contained in FAR Subpart 15.305.

Figure 25. Example of a Proposal Evaluation Process used by Federal Government

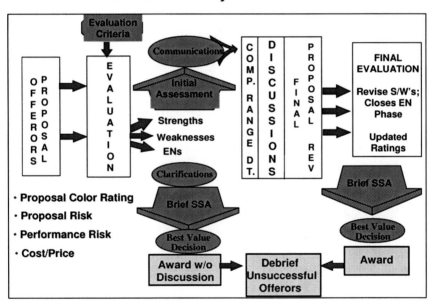

This chart is from a DOD procurement training session and resides in the public domain.

STEP 2-1:   Past Performance Evaluation

This section is important.   It's important because, on *Best-Value* contract awards, I've seen Past Performance weighed equally with both the technical and management portions of your proposal.   The weight given to Past Performance varies from agency to agency. When bidding a contract with the Air Force, for example, they mandate Past Performance will count for at least 25% of the award decision.   Government looks at your Past Performance in much the same way you would review the past performance of a Mutual Fund before deciding to buy it.   While the fund's past performance does not "guarantee" future performance, it is a good indication.

Past Performance information is obtained by a subset of the proposal evaluation team members who draw their information from three sources:

- **References provided by your company in the Past Performance Volume of your proposal**

- **Past Performance Information Retrieval System (PPIRS)**

- **References chosen by the Proposal Evaluators for further research into your Past Performance**

Obtaining *reference* information does not require a lot of time, but is sporadic with periods of lots of activity followed by waiting.   In fact, some RFPs ask that you submit Past Performance information in advance of the balance of your proposal so evaluators can begin sending out evaluation forms knowing it may take a while for the recipients to complete and return it.   Moreover, it may take a period of time to track down the PM, COR or others who are most familiar with your work.   It's worth your time to provide up-to-date contact information to government so they aren't using second-hand recommendations from a CO who only has the contract file on which to comment and no personal experience with your performance. This most often works to your disadvantage where on a scale of 1 to 5 (with 5 being the best); you'll probably receive a 3. So government follows up on your references by sending past PMs, CORs, COs and CSs an evaluation form to summarize their understanding of your Past Performance.

Past Performance Information Retrieval System or PPIRS is a web-enabled, government-wide application that serves as the central warehouse for contractor past performance assessment reports. It is sponsored by the DOD E-Business Office. PPIRS draws on information from the following sources:

- Contractor Performance System (CPS)

- Past Performance Data Base (PPBD)

- Past Performance Information Management System (PPIMS)

- Architect-Engineer Contract Administration Support System (ACASS)

- Construction Contractor Appraisal Support System (CCASS)

- Contractor Performance Assessment Reporting System (CPARS)

Depending on the product or service you sell to the government, you may have input documented in one or more of these databases. In the interest of fairness, you should have received a copy of any reports sent to one of these databases to provide you with an opportunity to comment. When the company PM has a superb working relationship with the COR, they may even review and discuss the report before it is processed through the CO and into the appropriate database. For more information on these data bases go to http://www.ppirs.gov/

Access to your report cards is allowed for individuals evaluating contractor proposals. Contractors may view their own data and can gain access through the Central Contractor Registration (CCR) process. A contractor must be registered in CCR and must have created a Marketing Partner Identification Number (MPIN) in the CCR profile to access their PPIRS information.

The SSEB Past Performance team may choose to *check references on other contracts* that surfaced through their research on PPIRS. Government, knowing the references you provided in your proposal were likely chosen because those projects went especially well, may choose to do this to give them a broader perspective on your performances.

So, it's the amalgamation of input from your references, PPIRS and government-initiated evaluations which result in a complete picture of past performance which yield your rating. This process is described in Figure 26. All of the information gathered above is evaluated for three factors: *Relevancy, Performance,* and *Confidence.*

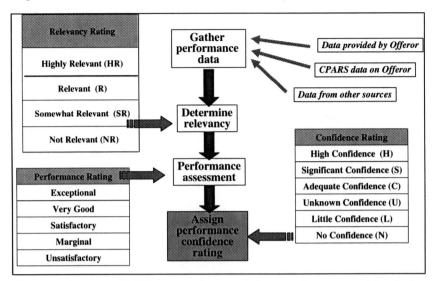

Figure 26. Past Performance Analysis Process

This chart is from a DOD procurement training session and resides in the public domain

Past Performance is reviewed by the evaluation team on two basic merits; relevancy and scope. Relevance means, "Is the contract you're bidding on similar in work to contracts you've worked on in the past?" Scope is the level of work you've contributed on past contracts that were similar to the contract you are now bidding.

Relevancy on a manufacturing contract can mean the level of technology you are using to produce circuit cards as replacement parts in a communication system. If the new contract calls for surface-mount components and you're still manufacturing using older technology it could be said your manufacturing capability is not relevant to the new contract. If you're bidding a professional service contract and have traditionally won government contracts providing administrative support people to perform routine business functions, such as timekeeping, scheduling conference rooms, and making power point slides, it could be said that level of work defines your niche. Although you may have an excellent reputation for providing such services, if the contract you're currently bidding requires you to provide PhD mathematicians and advanced-degree engineers, it could be said your past contract experience is not relevant to the contract you are bidding.

Scope is evaluated as part of Relevancy. It means, "Have you worked on contracts in the past that were similar to the level of effort of a new contract you are bidding?" Clearly, if the new contract requires a production rate of 100 circuit boards a month and your present capability is at 100 per year, there is a problem. If you historically supported contracts where you provided 5 people on contract per year and this new contract requires 50 people per year, you'll need to persuade the proposal evaluators you can scale up to support the new requirements. One way around this is to offer the government a plan in your proposal describing how your business processes are proven and scalable to the increased workload. This is intended to persuade government you can meet the demands of the new contract within the contract phase-in period of 30 days.

None of these shortfalls mean you cannot WIN the new contract, but it does mean your past experience places more risk on your perceived ability to perform. There are several ways around this dilemma. A popular approach is to describe the approach you will use on this contract to provide the surface-mount technology or higher level personnel to support this new contract. In essence you are closing the gap between the needs of the government and your existing capability.

Generally, the *Performance Metrics* described in the RFP will provide you with a first indication of the specific areas where you will be evaluated. These evaluations will be used by PPIRS.

Lastly, based upon your relevancy and performance scores on all contracts reviewed, government will assign an overall *Confidence Rating* of High, No Confidence, or something in between. At this point, seeing into this process and how much Past Performance counts in the overall decision on who receives the contract, explains why students in my training programs often comment, "The first thing I will do when I return to the office is clean up my Past Performance."

STEP 2-2:   Evaluation Summary

So where does all of this information from the technical/management, price/cost, and past performance go? One example is summarized in Table 14, Summary of Proposal Evaluations leading up to Contract Award. This is the "bottom line" that is presented to the Source Selection Authority (SSA), the decision maker who will review this information and determine which company will be awarded the contract. This briefing is delivered to the SSA by the PM managing this procurement through contract award. The column on the left summarizes all of the main points listed in the Evaluation Criteria (Section M of the RFP) by which your proposal was evaluated. Color coding, where blue denotes an outstanding evaluation of your proposal down to red for unacceptable, immediately tells the SSA that they could quickly eliminate Contractor 3 from further consideration because one area is unacceptable. This does not necessarily mean they cannot perform the work, but when compared with the other proposers; they impart an additional risk to the government.

Evaluation Factor	Contr. 1	Contr. 2	Contr. 3	Contr. 4
1: Past Performance	G	B	Y	B
2: Mission Capability				
2.1: Qualifications – Corporate Experience	B	B	G	B
2.2: Management	G	G	Y	G
3: Price/Cost	G	B	R	Y
4: Proposal Risk	G	G	Y	B

B	G	Y	R
Outstanding	Good	Marginal	Unacceptable

This chart is from a DOD procurement training session and resides in the public domain

As you can see, eliminating other contractors and arriving at who will ultimately WIN the contract is a huge subjective undertaking. At this point the details of your proposal evaluation come to light. All of your proposal strengths and your clarifications through ENs are used to comment and further clarify the overall color rating. This is where government "splits hairs" to determine who will ultimately WIN. On a separate note, it is these strengths, weaknesses, and your clarifying remarks that will serve as the narrative government will share with you in a Proposal Debrief should you request one after the Contract Award announcement is made.

STEP 2-3: Competitive Range Determination

When the SSEB completes their initial proposal review it may become apparent that one or more offerors is "outside the Competitive Range." This can mean a lot of things. It can mean your price is so high (or so low) as to cast doubt on your ability to compete with the other offerors. Sometimes a low Price/Cost may be explained in your other volumes. You may have a unique solution or technology to bring to this contract that allows you to pass the savings onto the government. Or, you may fall outside the competitive range because of other sections of your proposal. Regardless of the reason, it may not imply you have a bad proposal, it was simply not competitive with the others and this determination allows the government to save both you and themselves time and money pursuing an "unlikely" offer.

STEP 2-4: Preaward Debrief

Should your proposal be deemed to be outside the competitive range, you will be notified in writing by the Contracting Officer. The notice will state the basis for the determination and that proposal revisions will not be considered. You will have three business days to request a Preaward Debrief. While the government cannot share such information as the number of proposals, they will draw on their internal list of strengths and weaknesses from your proposal review to help you understand why you were eliminated from further consideration. This debrief is specifically designed to help you do better on future proposals.

STEP 3: Contract Award

When government decides which proposal won, they notify the WINner and the other offerors. The WINner is typically notified by a telephone call from the CO or CS congratulating them. In some instances, especially when it involves high dollar value or PRESS-worthy notoriety, the call may come from a Senator or Congressman directly to the company president. Offerors who did not win are notified by the Contracting Officer in writing stating their proposals were within the competitive range, but were not selected for award. This notice will include:

- The number of offerors solicited

- The number of proposals received

- The name and address of each offeror receiving a contract award

- The items, quantities and unit prices of each award

- In general terms, the reason why your proposal was not accepted.

Everyone else is told through a posting in FedBizOpps.

This concludes Chapter 11. Our next and final chapter is Chapter 12: Contract Negotiations and Your Proposal Debrief. It will describe the steps that occur within your company in parallel with Governments Phase B, Proposal Evaluation.

Chapter 12.0 Contract Negotiations and Proposal Debrief (Phase 3)

Chapter 12 is the last Phase in the Five-Phase Approach™ to Business Development. It is accomplished in parallel with Phase B in government where all proposals are being evaluated. Below we'll look more closely at the eight steps in Phase 3 and include comments and suggestions on how to interact with the client. Whether you WIN this particular contract or not, Phase 3 is one more step in helping cement your relationship with the client on both this and future procurement opportunities. It will also uncover important lessons learned on how you can improve your proposal submissions to this client and others.

The eight steps in Phase 3 are:

> STEP 1: Answer Questions
> STEP 2: Preaward Debrief
> STEP 3: Contract Negotiations
> STEP 4: Contract Award
> STEP 5: Proposal Debrief
> STEP 6: Protest
> STEP 7: Celebration!
> STEP 8: Kick-off Meeting

STEP 1: Answer Questions

Questions from the client during their proposal evaluation are called *Evaluation Notices* (ENs). As you recall from Phase B, when proposal evaluators are reading your proposal they make notes on what they especially liked (called strengths) and points that exhibited a weakness, or an unclear part of your proposal. It's these weaknesses or unclear portions of your proposal that become ENs that will require a response from you through the Contracting Officer.

There are two basic kinds of ENs: small and large. Small ENs are merely clarifications, or a request for you to correct an obvious error in your proposal. One example of a small EN is the heading in a table where it was labeled 'Man-Hours' and it was clearly intended to read 'Man-Years'. A large EN could require you to enter into discussions or negotiations with the government and may even require resubmission of an entire rewritten volume of your proposal. The significance of this big EN versus a small EN can mean the difference between the Government issuing a contract award in six weeks versus six months. These are two very different paths; quickly moving to award without negotiations versus the longer process of negotiations are the result of what's discovered from a first review of your proposal. The implications are more far reaching than just the time it takes to award the contract. It also means a lot more work for the Source Selection Evaluation Board (SSEB), and you. So the moral of the story is to be extremely clear and concise with your first proposal submission.

When you are assigned ENs, the first indication they are small is if you're given only 2 or 3 days to reply. With any size EN, it behooves you to reply as quickly as possible so the proposal evaluators can continue with their work. Your responsiveness is an important contributor to how government views you. Also, when replying to ENs make certain the response you return to the government has the same proprietary markings as on your original submission. Being responsive to the governments ENs is also an important step in *relationship maintenance* for future opportunities.

STEP 2: Preaward Debrief

When the CO notifies you that you have been excluded from the competitive range, it should be accompanied by a brief explanation of what eliminated your proposal from further consideration. At this point the CO won't ask for additional input, but you should be notified that you may request a Preaward Debrief. Be advised, it's your responsibility to ask for one and you must make this request within 3 working days of being notified.

Below is a list of what you can and cannot expect to learn from the debrief.

Debrief Includes	Does Not Include
• Significant Elements of your Proposal • Rationale for Elimination • Reasonable Answers to your Questions	• Number of Offerors • Identity of Offerors • Contents of Other Proposals • Ranking of Offerors • Evaluation of Others

Since obtaining a debrief is such an important step in *relationship maintenance*, your request should be presented with a tone that conveys you are searching for information that will help you do better in the future.

STEP 3: Contract Negotiations

Contract Negotiations may be conducted between your company representatives and a government negotiator. In some instances the CO or CS may serve as the negotiator. In attendance is also the SSEB Chairman who is the PM for this procurement. He/she is there to answer questions about the technical details of the procurement, but the person serving as the negotiator is in control of the meeting.

Negotiations with the Federal Government differ greatly from negotiations between two private companies. The big difference is what's open to negotiation. Should the negotiator raise a concern about the inclusion of certain expenses or the amount of the fee you added to your costs, a review of the FAR can quickly put such concerns to rest. This is not the case in company-to-company negotiations where the client may not care what your costs are when they are only willing to pay what has been budgeted for the product or service. This more demanding approach is also quite common when negotiating with national labs that are run by private companies. They can be tough negotiators.

It has been my experience that government frequently negotiates City Services contracts, that are price sensitive. In sharp contrast, contracts that support Core Functions are oftentimes awarded based on *Best Value*. In this case your price is but one, oftentimes small, factor where the client is willing to pay more for a superior level of technical performance or a new technology that promises a greater payoff later on.

STEP 4: Contract Award

As mentioned in Chapter 11, after government has decided which proposal won, they notify the winner, as well as the other offerors. The winner is notified by a telephone call from the CO or CS congratulating them. Offerors who did not win are notified by the Contracting Officer in writing stating their proposals were within the competitive range, but were not selected for award.

Everyone else is informed through a posting in FedBizOpps and includes:

- Number of Proposals

- Name and Address of Offeror(s) receiving contract

- Items, Quantity and Price of Each Award

This posting may serve as valuable intelligence for the Business Development Manager who is looking toward the future. Especially if this is a recurring contract, the solicitation, scope of work (or PWS), and dollar value of the award is advance information to help position your company for the follow-on contract.

STEP 5: Proposal Debrief

Conventional wisdom tells us that if we lost the contract we would request a debrief to better understand why we lost. *Proactive companies* request a debrief whether they WIN or lose and for the same reason, they want timely feedback on the content of their last proposal submission to help them in their very next proposal, regardless of who the client might be.

In sharp contrast to the Preaward Debrief that is run by someone from the Contracting Office, the Chairman of the SSEB (the PM) typically runs the proposal debrief to address all aspects of the evaluation. The SSA, CO, and CS are also present. Probably one of the first charts the SSEB Chairman will brief is the Evaluation Criteria, the "scorecard" your proposal was gauged against. Here, all of the strengths and weaknesses from the team's evaluation of all proposal volumes are summarized to deliver a factual accounting of what the offeror did especially well and where shortcomings were noticed. Let the government present and then ask questions when afforded the opportunity. These *pearls of wisdom* were bought with your valuable time. Take advantage of it. Information you should expect to learn includes the following:

You're Entitled to:

- Total Score received by the winner

- Summary of rationale for the Award

- Reasonable response to questions

- Name, title and responsibility of decision maker

Your Overall Evaluation—in each major area:

- Capabilities

- Past Performance

- Proposal Risk

- Cost or Price

Your debrief will not include a point-by-point comparison of *Your* Proposal with others, the strengths and weaknesses of each offeror, or specifics of the price and cost evaluation for yourself and other offerors. Also, you will not be able to see a copy of other proposals and the Government will *not* offer any information other than what is *required* unless you specifically ask.

This forum is intended to help the contractor do an even better job in their next proposal and the tone should be cordial. Superior companies know that at this stage they aren't going to change who was awarded this contract. Rather, they are using this opportunity to thank the government for their fair and impartial evaluation and are positive in their comments to use this valuable information to WIN the next contract.

After adjourning the meeting, add these lessons learned to your Resource Library for your next proposal.

STEP 6: Protest

This is an unsavory, but necessary topic. A Protest claims the Government violated a procurement regulation AND it is *so blatant that your lawyer agrees you have a substantial probability of winning.* I added the part about your lawyer because you need to know that only 10% of companies who file protests win; and of course the emotional and financial drain can last for years. Also, there are procedural mechanisms in place to diffuse the potential for protests. Earlier, in Section 8.4.10, I cited where the BRASS contract had an Ombudsman available. As you recall, this person has no authority, but can help you understand how the government procurement process works in the hopes it will help you vent and/or understand why some procedure was handled in a particular way.

I suggest that if you feel you were wronged, consider getting a debrief first and then speak with the CO before committing to a protest. For more information on protests you can turn to the FAR, Part 33, for guidance on this important subject.

"It's better to look forward than backward"

AUTHOR UNKNOWN

I suggest there are two kinds of celebrations: one after you are told you won the contract, and another smaller expression of your gratitude, after submitting the proposal. We all know how to celebrate if we just won a big contract, however, acknowledging the people who contributed long hours to make the last proposal deadline is sometimes overlooked.

To celebrate turning in an especially large or challenging proposal, I suggest bringing in some food, or at least a brief recognition over coffee, nothing big, but something to say thank you. You can easily go around the room and single out the contributors. One simple three-sentence formula I have used successfully is as follows:

Sentence 1

"This was Susan's first proposal with our company. In fact, it was her first proposal ever."

Sentence 2

"Whether it was proofing a 1 page input from an SME after hours or ensuring all last-minute changes had been made before going into production, she quickly became an indispensable member of our team."

Sentence 3

"Susan, we all look forward to your invaluable contribution and energy on future projects."

Remember, you may need some help with your next proposal. Below are some choice words that might help generate ideas for recognizing your people:

- Unwavering
- Positive mental attitude
- Responsive
- Lynchpin
- Par excellence
- Prized employee
- Privilege
- Professionalism
- Our Most Valuable Player (MVP)
- Uncommon energy
- Enthusiasm

STEP 8: Kick-off Meeting

When you WIN the contract, there will be a kick-off meeting with your team and the client. Typically, like the Proposal Debrief, its run by the PM for the solicitation and the Chairman of the SSEB. He/she now, after contract award, is probably the COR responsible for day-to-day interactions with your contract Program Manager.

In this meeting the proceedings will focus on congratulatory accolades followed by discussions intended to help you "hit the ground running" so you will be successful on this new contract. All of the details that didn't necessarily make it into the Proposal Debrief (if you asked for one) are openly discussed in this forum so everyone around the table understands the expectations for success.   This is yet another opportunity to begin this new relationship in the hopes it leads to many more successful ventures.

This concludes Phase 3 and the Five-Phase Approach^{TM} to Business Development. Be reminded from my earlier remarks that this book looked closely at one procurement action to help describe the processes, decision points and the structure of creating a WINning proposal. In reality, your pursuit of new business (Phase 1) is an ongoing process of uncovering new opportunities.

Closing Remarks

There is no greater pride than knowing you are responsible for bringing meaningful, billable work into your company. With our young men and women at war in a far away country we now see that behind every aircraft, every rebuilding project, every meal and every flight back home for a couple of weeks with the family, is the support of an army of prime and subcontractors. What you do is important. The objective of this book is to help you diversify into the federal marketplace or start your new business with a government contract. Reading this book has brought you one step closer.

I began this book with a statement that only 5 % of U.S. companies do business with the Federal Government. After reading these 12 chapters it should be clear that there are numerous ways to conduct profitable business with the government and national laboratories. Much of what you read may have sounded strikingly familiar from your private sector experience. The truly unique aspects of doing business with government are described in the Five-Phase Approach^{TM} to Business Development and the 17-Step approach to creating a WINning proposal. Now you can see that doing business with government is an achievable and noble undertaking.

Good Luck!

Appendix A - Glossary of Terms

Acquisition - The acquiring of supplies or services by the federal government through purchase or lease using appropriated funds.

Action Caption - A short informative statement with a graphic that provides additional information about the content of the graphic to help the reader draw the correct conclusion.

Acquisition Planning - Coordinating and integrating people responsible for an acquisition through a comprehensive plan for fulfilling the agency's need in a timely manner at a reasonable cost.

Benefit - A benefit in a proposal will resolve a customer issue. To claim a benefit, there must be a feature of the offer that clearly allows the benefit to be realized.

Best Value - In the Government's estimation, an acquisition that provides the greatest overall benefit to the requirement where price/cost is but one factor.

Boilerplate - Text and graphics that are stored so they are available for repeated use in multiple proposals.

Broad Agency Announcement (BAA) - A general announcement of an agency's research interest including criteria for selecting proposals.

Buyer - A professional purchaser, purchasing agent, procurement specialist etc. Buyers typically specialize in a given group of materials or services and are responsible for market analysis, purchase planning, and coordination with users.

Capture Strategy - A plan including documented analysis and follow-up actions necessary to pursue and win a specific opportunity.

Central Contractor Registration (CCR) database - The primary government repository for contractor information required for the conduct of business with the government. When the contractor has entered all mandatory information including the DUNS number into the CCR database the government will validate mandatory data and mark the record "Active."

Certified 8(a) Firm - A firm owned and operated by socially and economically disadvantaged individuals and are eligible to receive federal contracts under the Federal Government Small Business Administration's 8(a) Business Development Program.

Commercial-Off-The-Shelf (COTS) - Refers to supplies readily available in the commercial marketplace and requires no unique modification.

Competitive Analysis (or Bidder Comparison) - A tool used to compare a potential offer against possible competitor offers as judged by the customer.

Competitive Negotiation - A method for purchasing products and services, usually of a highly complex and technical nature whereby qualified individuals or vendors are solicited by means of a Request for Proposals (RFPs). Negotiations are conducted with selected offerors, the best proposal, as judged against criteria contained in the Request for Proposals, is accepted, and an award issued.

Requirement Matrix - Also called a compliance matrix. The matrix is a road map that enables the evaluator to easily you're your reply to requirements throughout the proposal.

Contract - A mutually binding legal relationship obligating the seller to furnish the products or services and the buyer to pay for them.

Contract Administration - The management of all facets of a contract to assure the vendor's total performance is in accordance with the contractual commitments and that the obligation of the vendor under the terms and conditions of the contract are fulfilled.

Contract Administration Office (CAO) - The organization assigned responsibility for ensuring that the contractor complies with the terms and conditions of the contract.

Contracting Activity - an office in an agency that is delegated broad authority regarding acquisition functions as designated by the head of that agency.

Contracting Office - an office that awards or executes a contract for supplies or services and performs post-award functions.

Contracting Officer - a person with the authority to enter into, administer, and/or terminate contracts, and make related determinations and findings.

Contract Officer (CO), Contract Specialist (CS), Buyer - An agency employee whose primary assignment is purchasing products or services with signature authority to commit the government to expend federal funds.

Contracting Officer's Representative (COR) - A subject matter expert who often performs inspection of contractor services on behalf of a government agency and the contracting officer.

Contractor - An individual or vendor that has entered into an agreement to provide products or services to an agency.

Contract Specialist (CS) – An individual who executes and administers contracts for the procurement of products, services, construction, or research and development. Tasks involve the use of formal advertising or negotiation methods, evaluation of contract price/cost proposals, administration or termination and close-out of contracts, and the development of policies and procedures for contracting/procurement work.

Cost or Pricing Data - All facts that, as of the date of price agreement, prudent buyers and sellers would reasonably expect to affect price negotiations significantly. Cost or pricing data are factual, not judgmental, and are verifiable.

Cost Plus Award Fee Contracts (CPAF) - The pricing structure of a contract in which the contractor is reimbursed for all allowable, allocable and "reasonable" costs. The contract typically will include a base fee, and an award fee as an incentive for superior performance.

that provides for payment to the contractor of a negotiated fee that is fixed at the inception of the contract. The fixed fee does not vary with actual cost, but may be adjusted as a result of changes in the work to be performed under the contract.

Cost- Plus Incentive Fee (CPIF) - A cost-reimbursement contract that provides for the initially negotiated fee to be adjusted later by a formula based on the relationship of total allowable costs to total target costs. This contract type specifies a target cost, a target fee, minimum and maximum fees, and a fee adjustment formula. After contract performance, the fee payable to the contractor is determined in accordance with the formula.

Cost Reimbursement Contracts – A contract based on payment by an agency to a contractor of allowable, reasonable and allocable costs incurred in the contract performance to the extent prescribed in the contract. The contract may not require completion of the contract work, but rather the best efforts of the contractor. Types of cost reimbursement contracts include: (a) cost, (b) cost sharing, (c) cost plus fixed fee (CPFF), (d) cost-plus incentive fee (CPIF), and (e) cost plus award fee (CPAF).

Critical Path Method (CPM) - A system of project planning, scheduling, and control which combines all relevant information into a single master plan, permitting the establishment of the optimum sequence and duration of activities; shows the interrelation of all the efforts required to complete a construction project; and indicates the efforts which are critical to timely completion of the project.

Customer Profile - A maintained record of the characteristics of a customer. The profile may be used from bid to bid and can provide useful background information.

Data Universal Numbering System (DUNS) Number – A unique 9-digit number assigned by Dun and Bradstreet, Inc. (D&B), to identify unique business entities.

Davis-Bacon Wages - Wage determinations issued by the Department of Labor to specify the minimum wage rates to pay on federally funded or assisted construction projects. It represents the prevailing wage rate corresponding to the union wage and also reflects wages in urban areas where union membership tends to be higher.

Defense Contract Audit Agency (DCAA) – The government agency that performs all contract audits for the Department of Defense, providing accounting and financial advisory services regarding contracts and subcontracts to all DOD components responsible for procurement and contract administration. These services are provided in connection with negotiation, administration, and settlement of contracts and subcontracts.

Direct Cost - Any cost that is identified specifically with a particular final cost objective. Direct costs are not limited to items that are incorporated in the end product as material or labor. Costs identified specifically with a contract are direct costs of that contract.

Discriminator - A unique feature in a proposal that supports a benefit.

Electronic Data Interchange (EDI) - Transmission of information between computers using standardized electronic versions of common business documents.

Executive Summary - A short summary of the main points of the offer aimed at the senior level decision makers in the customer's organization.

Features - Tangible aspects of the proposal. They are normally measurable and demonstrable.

FedBizOpps.gov (FBO) - The single government point-of-entry (GPE) for federal government procurement opportunities over $25,000. Government buyers publicize their business opportunities by posting directly to the Internet. Commercial vendors seeking federal markets for their products and services can search, monitor and retrieve opportunities solicited by the entire federal contracting community.

Federal Acquisition Regulations (FAR) - The body of regulations that are the primary sources of authority governing the federal government procurement process.

Federal Supply Schedule (FSS) Program - A "simplified" process for procuring commonly used supplies or services by placing delivery orders against Federal Supply Schedule contracts that have been awarded by the General Services Administration (GSA) for use by numerous federal agencies.

Fixed Price Contract - A type of contract that provides for a firm price or, under appropriate circumstances, for an adjustable price for the products or services being procured.

Freedom of Information Act (FOIA) - The Freedom of Information Act of 1966 protects the rights of the public to information and makes provisions for individuals to obtain information on the operation of federal agencies.

Full and Open Competition – Competition in which all responsible sources are permitted to compete on a contract action.

General and Administrative (G&A) Expense - Any management, financial, and other expense which is incurred by or allocated to a business unit for the general management and administration of the business unit as a whole.

Ghosting – Exploiting a competitors weakness by highlighting it as a strength in your proposal.

Hot Buttons - Singularly important issues or set of issues that are likely to drive decisions, usually associated with customer buying decisions.

HUB Zone - An historically underutilized business zone or area located within one or more qualified census tracts, qualified non-metropolitan counties, or lands within the external boundaries of an Indian reservation.

HUB Zone Small Business - A small business concern that appears on the List of Qualified HUB Zone Small Business maintained by the Small Business Administration.

Indefinite Delivery/Indefinite Quantity Contracts (ID/IQ): A type of contract in which the exact date of delivery or the exact quantity are not specified until a delivery or task order is issued.

Indirect Cost - Any cost not directly identified with a single final cost objective, but identified with two or more final cost objectives or with at least one intermediate cost objective.

Indirect Cost Rate - The percentage or dollar factor that expresses the ratio of indirect expense incurred in a given period to direct labor cost, manufacturing cost, or another appropriate base for the same period.

Inherently Governmental Function - A function that, as a matter of policy, is so intimately related to the public interest as to mandate performance by government employees.

Issues - Concerns of the customer that require resolution by the bidder. Issues may be emotional and not articulated in the customer's requirement documents.

Joint Venture - An association of two or more business entities to carry on a single business enterprise for profit, and for which purpose they combine their property, capital, efforts, skills and knowledge.

Kick-off Meeting – a meeting that serves to initiate a proposal effort for all contributors, answer questions about an opportunity, make writing assignments, coordinate upcoming activities, and create a cohesive team.

Market Research – Collection and analysis of information about capabilities within the market to satisfy agency needs.

Market Survey - An attempt to determine the availability of qualified sources capable of satisfying an agency's procurement requirements. This testing of the marketplace may range from written or telephone contacts with knowledgeable experts regarding similar or duplicate requirements, and the results of any market test recently undertaken, to the more formal sources-sought announcements in pertinent publications (e.g., technical/scientific journals, or the FedBizOpps, or Requests for Information (RFIs) for planning purposes.

National Nuclear Security Administration (NNSA) - A semi-autonomous agency within the U.S. Department of Energy that was established by Congress in 2000. The NNSA is responsible for enhancing national security through the military application of nuclear energy, and maintaining and enhancing the safety, security, reliability and performance of the U.S. nuclear weapons stockpile.

North American Industrial Classification System or "NAICS": (pronounced "Nakes") - New codes developed by the Census Bureau to replace the current SIC Code. NAICS recognize hundreds of new businesses in our economy, primarily in the fast growing service sector. NAICS classifications are updated regularly to keep pace with changing business conditions and information needs. The new numbering system provides five levels of classification containing detailed codes that have a maximum of six digits.

Offer - A response to a solicitation that, if accepted, would bind the offeror to perform the resulting contract. Responses to invitations for bids (sealed bidding) are offers called "bids" or "sealed bids"; responses to Requests for Proposals (negotiated contracts) are offers called "proposals"; however, responses to requests for quotations (simplified acquisition) are "quotations," not offers.

Offeror – bidder.

Online Representations and Certifications Application (ORCA) - The primary government repository for representations and certifications submitted by the contractor that are required for the conduct of business with the government. ORCA is part of the Business Partner Network (BPN).

Option - A unilateral right in a contract by which, for a specified time, the government may elect to purchase additional products or services called for by the contract, or may elect to extend the term of the contract.

Performance-Based Contracting - Structuring an acquisition around objective measurable outcomes rather than broad and imprecise Statements of Work (SOW).

Performance Based Service Acquisition (PBSA) – Also referred to as performance-based contracting or performance contracting. A variety of acquisition strategies, methods, and techniques that describe and communicate measurable outcomes rather than direct performance processes. Such contracts are structured around defining a service requirement in terms of performance objectives and providing contractors the latitude to determine how to meet those objectives, i.e. it is a method for purchasing what is required and placing the responsibility for how it is accomplished by the contractor. In some cases, for example in energy retrofits, the contractor can be paid based upon the amount of money saved.

Performance Work Statement (PWS) - A method for the agency to articulate its requirement, and is used in PBSA (see Performance Based Service Acquisition above). Sometimes called a performance-based SOW.

Past Performance Information Retrieval System (PPIRS) - The central warehouse for contractor past performance assessment reports. Government access is restricted to individuals evaluating contractor proposals. Contractors may view their own data through the Central Contractor Registration (CCR) process. A contractor registered in CCR and must have a Marketing Partner Identification Number (MPIN) in the CCR profile to access their PPIRS information. Website: http://www.ppirs.gov/

Pre-Award Survey - An evaluation by an agency representative of a prospective contractor's capability to perform a proposed contract. Can include site visit to contractor facilities etc.

Pre-Bid Conference or Pre-Bid Walk-Through – A meeting held with prospective bidders or offerors prior to submission of bids or proposals, to review, discuss, and clarify technical considerations, specifications, and standards relative to the proposed procurement.

Pre-Qualifications - A procedure to pre-qualify products or vendors and limit consideration of bids or proposals to only those products or vendors that have been pre-qualified.

Price - The amount of money that will purchase a definite amount of a commodity.

Pricing - The process of establishing a reasonable amount to be paid for products or services.

Prime Contractor - A corporation, partnership, business association, trust, joint-stock company, education institution or other non-profit organization, or individual who has entered into a prime contract with an agency.

Prime Contract - A contract between the government and a contractor (Prime Contractor) where other contractors are in a subordinate role supporting the Prime Contractor and are responsive to their direction being once removed from direct interactions with the government.

Procurement - The procedures for obtaining products or services, including all activities from the planning steps, preparation and processing of a requisition, through receipt, acceptance of delivery and the processing of a final invoice for payment.

Procurement Technical Assistance Centers (PTAC) – PTACs provide marketing and technical assistance to companies within your state or local community who are interested in selling products and services to federal, state and local governments. Their objective is to create jobs and expand the economy by providing specific, valuable low and no-cost training and informational resources to businesses. The Defense Logistics Agency (DLA), on behalf of the Secretary of Defense, administers the DOD Procurement Technical Assistance Program (PTAP), which sponsors these local resources.

Program Evaluation Review Technique (PERT) - This is a graphical means to plan, progress and track tasks in a project.

Program Manager in a Government Source Selection – The title assigned to a person who has the responsibility to assemble or develop requirements leading up to the award of a contract. He/she formulates the contract budget estimate and the milestones necessary to award the contract on time and represent the contract action before the Source Selection Authority (SSA), Contracting Office and the public.

Project Manager or Program Manager in the Private Sector – A person responsible for interacting with the client to translate goals into manageable and tractable milestones and budget items so the project/program can be accurately tracked and reported to the client and company management. He/she is also responsible for daily management of the project/program as well as identification and resolution of issues as they arise.

Proposal - A document used by an agency to evaluate the professional capabilities of a business, agency, or individual against a set of pre-established criteria that may be weighted using a set of questions that allows the agency to determine the best business, agency, or individual to hire for a specific job. The proposal is designed to evaluate such criteria as: previous work experience; work with the organization and specifically your program; whether preference can be given to local or in-state business; the qualifications of the lead professional and the qualifications of the team that will be working on the project; and if previous work has been completed on time and within budget.

Proposal Manager - Person responsible for: proposal development, including maintaining schedules; coordinating inputs, reviews, strategy and theme implementation; resolving internal problems; and providing process leadership.

Proposal Outline - A structure for a proposal that is derived from the customer's requirements. The outline may be annotated to show writing responsibilities, page count estimates and so on.

Proposal Process – A systematic series of steps directed toward WINning RFP's.

Proposal Schedule - A task based plan that identifies the period of time that effort is required for each task.

Protest - A written complaint about an administrative action or decision brought by a bidder or offeror to the appropriate administrative section with the intention of receiving a remedial result.

Public Bid Opening - The process of opening and reading bids at the time and place specified in the RFQ and in the presence of anyone who wishes to attend.

Quotation (or Quote) - A vendor statement of current prices in response to a Request For Quotation (RFQ). A quote is not considered an offer that could bind the quoter to a contract if accepted.

Reasonable Price - A price that does not exceed that which would be incurred by a prudent person in the conduct of a competitive business. Reasonable price can be established by market test, price or cost analysis, or the experience and judgment of the purchaser.

Request for Proposals (RFP) - All documents used for soliciting proposals. The RFP procedure usually requires negotiation with offerors as distinguished from competitive bidding when using an invitation for bids.

Red Team – A team who evaluates a draft proposal for customer focus, completeness and clear communication of the WIN strategy and solution by people who are independent of the proposal team and offer different perspectives; typically composed of experts on the customer, the customer's industry, competitors, the organization, technology, approach, and on preparing and presenting WINning proposals.

Red Team Review - Review to evaluate the proposal for customer focus, completeness and clear communication of the WIN Theme and solution by people who are independent of the proposal team.

Request for Quotation (RFQ) - A type of solicitation used typically with small dollar contracts or purchase, but may be used for commercial items up to an agency's prescribed dollar limit.

Service Contract - A contract for work performed by an independent vendor in which the service rendered does not consist primarily of the acquisition of equipment or materials, or the rental of equipment, materials and supplies.

Service-Disabled Veteran-Owned (SDVO) - A small business concern not less than 51 % owned by one or more service-disabled veterans; or, in the case of any publicly owned business, not less than 51 % of its stock is owned by one or more service-disabled veterans; and the management and daily business operations are controlled by one or more service-disabled veterans or, in the case of a veteran with permanent and severe disability, the spouse or permanent caregiver of such veteran. Service-disabled veteran means a veteran with a disability that is service-connected.

Scope of Work – A statement which provides bidders with a clear, accurate, and complete description of the work to be performed, including inspection, test and acceptance (see Statement of Work).

Set-aside - A contract designated for small or minority business bidding only.

Simplified Acquisition - The methods prescribed in Part 13 of the FAR for making purchases of supplies or services as determined by the head of the agency up to: (1) $250,000 for any contract to be awarded and performed inside the United States and (2) $1 million for any contract to be awarded and performed outside the United States. Simplified Acquisitions are processed on an *accelerated timeline* which can result in contract awards in months rather that the typical one and a half years typically associated with the government's processing of a Procurement action from Definition of Requirements through Contract Award.

Sole Source - A product or service that is practicably available from only one source.

Sole Source Acquisition - A contract for the purchase of products or services that is made by soliciting and negotiating with only one contractor.

Solicitation - An invitation for bids, a Request for Proposal (RFP), Request for Quote (RFQ), telephone calls, or any other document issued by the governmental entity to obtain bids or proposals for the purpose of entering into a contract.

Source Selection Authority (SSA) - Usually used in federal contracting, the SSA is the official designated to direct the source selection process, approve the selection plan, select the source(s), and announce the contract award.

Source Selection Evaluation Board (SSEB) - A group of military and/or government civilian personnel, representing functional and technical disciplines, charged with evaluating proposals and developing summary facts and findings during source selection.

Source Selection Information - Any information that is prepared for use by an agency for the purpose of evaluating a bid or proposal to enter into an agency procurement contract, if that information has not been previously made available to the public or disclosed.

Source Selection Sensitive – Any information prepared by the government in anticipation of awarding a contract which, if not released to all potential bidders, could give one bidder an unfair advantage.

Statement of Work (SOW) - That portion of the contract that clearly and concisely defines requirements of the specific work to be accomplished. Statements of work are individually tailored to consider the period of performance, deliverable items, if any, and the desired degree of performance flexibility. In the case of task order contracts, the statement of work for the basic contract only defines the scope of the overall contract in general terms. The statement of work for each task order must articulate the specific requirement.

Storyboard – A conceptual planning tool used to help writers plan each section before drafting text. It contains assignments, bid request requirements, strategies, theme points, preliminary visuals, and contents.

Subcontract - An agreement between a prime or general contractor and a subcontractor for the execution of a portion of the contractual obligation of the prime contract with the client.

Subcontracting Plan - A written plan, submitted by a prime contractor and approved by a contracting officer, which describes goals and actions the contractor plans to take to use small and small disadvantaged businesses to the maximum practicable extent in performing the contract.

Technical Proposal - An un-priced proposal that sets forth in detail what a vendor proposes to furnish in a response to a solicitation.

Terms And Conditions - Applied to the rules under which all bids/proposals must be submitted and the stipulations included in most purchase contracts; often published by the purchasing authorities for the information of all potential vendors.

Theme (or WIN Theme) - A short articulation to the proposal team during proposal development, and ultimately to the client, of the main point in a proposal. Typically, the theme would link a discriminating feature to a benefit.

Time and Material Contract - A contract providing for the procurement of supplies or services on the basis of direct labor hours at specified fixed hourly rates and material at cost, or at some bid percentage discount from manufacturer's catalog or list prices.

Unsolicited Proposal - A written proposal for a new or innovative idea that is submitted to an agency on the initiative of the offeror or for the purpose of obtaining a contract with the Government, and that is not in response to a request for proposal, Broad Agency Announcement (BAA), Small Business Innovation Research (SBIR) topic, Small Business Technology Transfer Research (STTR) topic, Program Research and Development Announcement, or any other government-initiated solicitation or program.

Value Engineering - An organized effort to analyze the functions of systems, equipment, facilities, services, and supplies for achieving the required functions at the lowest life-cycle cost consistent with required performance, reliability, quality, and safety.

Work Breakdown Structure (WBS) - Deliverable-oriented grouping of project elements that organizes and defines the total work scope of the project; each descending level represents an increasingly detailed definition of the project work.

Warrant - An official document which designates an individual as a contracting officer and states the limits of their authority.

Appendix B - List of Resources

Technical Management Consortium, Inc. - Speaking, Training, Consulting and Products by *Joseph Jablonski* on the topics of Government Contracting, Proposal Writing and Competitive Positioning. Visit our Website at www.proposalw.com for a listing of upcoming public workshops, web seminars, products and FREE Downloads.

Association Of Proposal Management Professionals (APMP) - Provides networking and education through professional symposia, conferences and publications: *The Perspective* and *Journal of the Association of Proposal Management Professionals*. Membership includes proposal and business development professionals engaged in a wide range of activities including *business development and acquisition, proposal management, program management, strategic planning, proposal consulting* and *proposal production.* These professionals come from a cross section of industries and employers that include: *Aerospace/Defense/Federal Contractors, Business/Industry/Commercial, Academia, Government, Non-Profit* and *Health Care.* Website: www.apmp.org

Air Force Office of Small and Disadvantaged Businesses - Marketing resource for long range plans including Small Business Innovative Research (SBIR) contracts or grants. Website: http:/sellairforce.org

Central Contractor Registry (CCR) – Registers your company and selects National American Industry Classification System (NAICS) Codes. Website: http://www.ccr.gov/

Department of Energy (DOE) Research - DOE Budget Documents by Organization, National Laboratory and State. Website: http://www.cfo.doe.gov/budget/07budget/Start.htm

DOE National Laboratory Website:
http://www.energy.gov/organization/labs-techcenters.htm

FedBizOpps.gov - The single government point-of-entry (GPE) for federal government procurement opportunities over $25,000. Government buyers publicize their business opportunities by posting directly to the Internet. Commercial vendors seeking federal markets for their products and services can search, monitor and retrieve opportunities solicited by the entire federal contracting community. Website: http://www.fedbizopps.gov/

Federal Acquisition Regulation (FAR) Website:
http://www.arnet.gov/far/

Freedom of Information Act (FOIA) - A listing of all federal agencies FOIA contacts – a real time saver! Website:
http://www.usdoj.gov/04foia/foiacontacts .htm

Government Small and Disadvantaged Business Website:
http://www.selltoairforce.org/Library/pdfs/websites.pdf

Los Alamos National Laboratory Supply Chain Management Website: http://www.business.lanl.gov

National Defense Industrial Association (NDIA) – America's leading Defense Industry association promoting National Security. The association provides individuals from academia, government, the military services, small businesses, prime contractors, and the international community, the opportunity to network effectively with the government - industry team, keep abreast of the latest in technology developments, and address and influence issues as well as government policies critical to the health of the defense industry. The association offers the opportunity to increase knowledge and contacts, and hear from the movers and shakers in the various fields through its network of divisions and chapters and over 80 technical and policy symposia and convention-exhibit programs each year. Website: http://ndia.org

National Laboratories - The U.S. Department of Energy manages twelve National Labs and 9 technology centers across the country. Website: http://www.energy.gov/organization/labs-techcenters.htm

National Contract Management Association (NCMA) - A professional association formed in 1959 to foster the professional growth and educational advancement of its members. As a membership-based, professional society, its leadership is composed of volunteer elected officers and one full-time staff person. Website: http://www.ncmahq.org

North American Industry Classification - An introduction to the North American Industry Classification System (NAICS). Website: http://www.ntis.gov

Online Representations and Certifications Application (ORCA) - The primary government repository for representations and certifications submitted by the contractor that are required for the conduct of business with the government. Website: http://orca.bpn.gov

Professional Aerospace Contractors Association (PACA) - of New Mexico was formed in 1984 to promote a healthy relationship between the aerospace industry and NM government agencies. It co-hosts with government a briefing for Industry in August of each year, as well as monthly luncheons with guest speakers, and special seminars on current topics related to doing business with government. Website: http://www.pacanm.org/

The **Project Management Institute (PMI®)** is the world's leading association for the project management profession. It administers a globally recognized, rigorous, education, and/or professional experience and examination-based professional credentialing program. Website: www.pmi.org

Proposal Graphics - The 24 Hour Company...*bid-winning proposal graphics*
6521 Arlington Blvd, Suite 501, Falls Church, VA 22042
For more information: Colleen Jolly, Principal colleen@24hrco.com
Phone: (703) 533-7209 FAX: (703) 533-3959 Website: www.24hrco.com

Proposal Print-on-Demand (POD) and distribution services available through Mimeo in Knoxville, TN. Mimeo.com has built one of the world's largest automated digital printing facilities on FedEx's North American hub. Their online technology allows you to click "print" from your computer directly to their printers so you can print, bind, and deliver customized documents in the sequence you want them, add customized tabs, and select the binding of your choice. As long as you hit "print" prior to 10pm EST, your documents will arrive where you specify by the next morning according to FedEx's delivery schedule. They require no contracts or minimum orders and are a great complement to your internal system for overage or last minute projects. Website: http://www.mimeo.com/

Procurement Technical Assistance Center (PTAC) - PTACs provide marketing and technical assistance to companies within your state or local community who are interested in selling products and services to federal, state and local governments. Their objective is to create jobs and expand the economy by providing specific, valuable low and no-cost training and informational resources to businesses. The Defense Logistics Agency (DLA), on behalf of the Secretary of Defense, administers the DOD Procurement Technical Assistance Program (PTAP), which sponsors these local resources. Website: http://www.dla.mil/db/procurem.htm to look up the PTACs in your state.

Sandia National Laboratories Procurement: Website: http://www.sandia.gov/supplier/

Small Business Administration (SBA) Website: http://www.sba.gov/

Websites to Help with Grammar - http://www.webgrammar.com
http://www.grammarlady.com/faq.html
http://englishplus.com/grammar/

Work Break Down Structure (WBS) - A common project management tool used to document the scope of a project and break it into smaller elements that are easily planned and tracked. The WBS becomes a hierarchical "tree diagram" dividing larger parts of a project into its smaller, contributing elements. Website: http://www.hyperthot.com/pm_wbs.htm

Index

274

ORDER FORM
Technical Management Consortium, Inc.

First Name _____ MI ___

Last Name _____

Title _____

Company _____

Address _____

_____

City_____

State_____ Zip _____

Phone_____

FAX _____

Email _____

How did your hear about us? _____

_____

ORDER may be submitted:

1. **Online** at:
   www.proposalw.com

2. **Fax** to: (866) 908-1877
   Available 24 hours a day,
   everyday!!

3. **Emailed** to:
   info@proposalw.com

4. **Mailed** to:
   Technical Management
   Consortium, Inc.
   1708 White Cloud NE
   Albuquerque, NM 87112

For questions you may email
info@proposalw.com or
Call 505-270-1080.

Please Check One Preferred Method of Payment

☐ Visa   ☐ MasterCard   ☐ AMEX   ☐ Diners Club

Card Number _____

Exp. Date _____

Cardholder's Signature _____

☐ Check Enclosed in the amount of $ _____

Item Description	Price Each	Qty. Ordered	Total for Qty. Ordered
Proposal Writing to WIN Book	$40.		
Gross Receipts Tax for NM Residents at 6.9% =			
Shipping & Handling =			$7.00
Total Charges =			

We also offer *Speaking, Training and Consulting Services.*
www.proposalw.com

Printed in the United States
77038LV00002B/199-258